FROM SLATES TO LAPTOPS

FROM SLATES TO LAPTOPS

Memoirs of a Primary School Teacher

Elizabeth Forth

Central Print Services
University of Hull

Acknowledgements

My thanks to Richard Burkitt at 'For The Right Reasons' who encouraged me to write this memoir.

To the group of 'Writers at …' for giving me the confidence to persevere.

Grateful thanks also to Linda Wilson, Carol McCoid, Lynne Emmerson and Sonia Cameron Jacks for their support and comments.

First Published and Printed
by
For The Right Reasons
Inverness 2017

Re-produced by Central Print Services
University of Hull 2018

Copyright © Elizabeth Forth
2017

The names of all pupils and schools described in this memoir have been altered or omitted in order to protect privacy.

Contents

INTRODUCTION	Back to School	1
PART 1	**Pre-Teaching Experience**	3
	Slates	4
Chapter 1	My own School Education 1952-1964	5
Chapter 2	Teacher Training 1968-1971	15
PART 2	**Life in an Inner City Primary School**	21
Chapter 3	Baptism of Fire	22
Chapter 4	Setting the Scene	24
Chapter 5	The Children	34
Chapter 6	The Basic Skills	47
Chapter 7	The First Year Draws to a Close	52
Chapter 8	A New School Year	54
Chapter 9	Another School Year	66
Chapter 10	A New Headteacher: A New Regime	70
PART 3	**New Horizons**	91
Chapter 11	The Country Schools	94
Chapter 12	Back to Full Time Teaching	98
Chapter 13	A Change of School	102
Chapter 14	Secondment	108
Chapter 15	Back to School	113
Chapter 16	Curriculum Development Officer	118
Chapter 17	Acting Depute Head	122
Chapter 18	New Innovations	125
Chapter 19	Lecturer in Primary Development	132
PART 4	**A new Challenge**	137
Chapter 20	The Private Sector	148
SUMMARY		154

INTRODUCTION

Back To School

Five decades may seem like a long time, but to those of us who are now so generously referred to as 'Senior Citizens' it is but a fleeting moment.

This memoir is about my experience in education, from my own schooldays in the 1950s and 1960s through my career as a primary school teacher stretching over 30 years into the new millennium; it covers 50 years of unprecedented change in education.

Within the primary classroom it is possible to see into the heart of education, the children themselves. This insight highlights the behaviour displayed by pupils as, in some cases, they struggle to adapt to the system. I taught children from across the whole social spectrum and no matter what their circumstances they are all special; they all have their needs but, for some, the problems are such that they must be addressed before the learning process can even begin.

Aside from the challenges faced by the children themselves, teachers have also faced challenges, mostly brought about by changes in education, often imposed too quickly and without adequate support: pressures, which undoubtedly, in turn, impacted on the pupils. Over the decades these changes have been enormous, and it is within the classroom itself that we see how a serious lack of understanding on the part of those who endeavour to instruct the profession can adversely affect the whole system.

Maybe in order to move forward effectively we need to take a look back.

PART 1

PRE-TEACHING EXPERIENCE

SLATES

My mum was a real storyteller. Often, as we sat around the table for dinner, she would relate tales from her own childhood.

In her schooldays, between the two World Wars, children wrote on slates using a slate pencil.

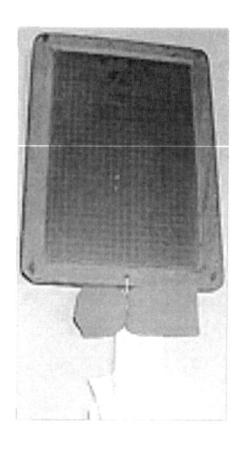

The writing slate consisted of a piece of slate, which was encased in a wooden frame. A piece of cloth or slate sponge was used to clean it and this was sometimes attached with a string to the bottom of the writing slate.

One day Mum got some of her sums wrong so the teacher hit her over the head with the slate. Now, at that time a child would rarely tell their parents if they had been in trouble at school for, invariably, it would result in further punishment at home. However, apart from being upset, Mum was physically sick. When my Gran, who was a real force to be reckoned with, extricated the truth from her she was very angry and hastened straight to the school to confront the teacher. It never happened again!

Slates continued to be in use during the Second World War and into the 1950s, as I remember from my own early school days, although chalk rather than a slate pencil was probably the more usual writing implement.

CHAPTER 1
My Own School Education 1952 - 1964

On my fifth birthday in May my mother took me along to the local infant school hoping that I would be enrolled immediately. Not so, I had to return in September at the beginning of the new school term. At that time there were three intakes of children throughout the school year. These occurred at the beginning of each of the three school terms: Autumn, Spring and Summer.

When the big day finally arrived my 'little sister', some 17 months younger than me, pushed me down the stairs: she wanted to go to school too. Not the best start to the day!

On arrival at the school we were directed to a classroom along with the many other new entrants and their parents. After introducing ourselves to the teacher who was seated behind a large desk, parents departed and there we were, in a class of 70. How on earth it was possible for one adult to cater for that number of pupils is beyond me. However, we were generally a very well behaved bunch, aside from one boy who was always in trouble. I have a vivid memory of him being yanked into the classroom by the scruff of the neck by the Headmistress and held as an example to us all. The number of pupils in the classes gradually reduced over the years, down to 50 by the time I reached the final junior school year at the age of ten.

In the reception class the desks were arranged in tables: we were very cramped. There was a Wendy House in the corner but it was a huge privilege to be allowed into it. For the most part we stayed in our seats, in any case there was hardly room to move about. The room was heated by a coal fire from which we were protected by a large fireguard.

Throughout my years in the infant and junior school class lessons were conducted by the teacher from the front of the room. The basic curriculum consisted of 'The Three R's' ('reading, 'riting, 'rithmetic): Reading, Writing and Arithmetic. We would all read from the same page of the same reading book at the same time. Apart from the 'Janet and John' reading books I don't remember any other commercially produced materials. In Arithmetic we chanted the multiplication tables and worked through 'sum' cards produced by the class teacher. Group teaching was simply not an option with so many in the class but somehow we managed to learn, and remarkably well at that. In Writing, as we progressed through the Junior School, we were expected to write stories but given little or no guidance on the subject matter, simply told to, "write about...", with perhaps a few words written up on the blackboard. All very well for children with vivid imaginations but I suspect that most, like myself, were left floundering. We were never given any homework.

On my first day at school my mum came to take me home at dinnertime. I was most indignant and, in a bid for independence, told her if she came to pick me up again I would not go back to school any more. Things were so different in those days. It was a $^3/_4$ mile walk to school but the lunch break was $1^1/_2$ hours, and as most children went home this allowed plenty of time. Lots of other children lived near to us so there was always plenty of company and, with no main roads to cross and little traffic, we were safe enough.

The majority of mums stayed at home and even some fathers came home for dinner at mid-day. It was the main meal of the day.

There was only one occasion throughout my childhood when I was late for school. Somehow Mum had managed to lock herself out of the house in the morning and had to go to Dad's work to get his key. Consequently the meal was late and I was late returning to school, although only by a few minutes. I was made to stand in front of the class and was smacked. I thought this was very unfair: I was scarcely six years old.

Life was very different in the 1950s. One of the greatest joys of childhood was 'going out to play'. We had much more freedom; we were not under constant observation by adults; there was little traffic and none of the distractions of the technological age. Although in school we were very cramped for space we did have PE lessons in the hall each week, and walking a total of three miles to and from school each day together with almost all of our spare time spent outside playing, we had plenty of exercise. Food was plain but nutritious and sweets were a luxury. Obesity was almost non-existent: The few children who were overweight were recognised as having serious medical problems.

As can be seen, we enjoyed a healthy balance of activity and study. In the classroom we worked, the rest of the time was 'ours'.

After just one term in the reception class we joined different classes 'streamed' according to ability. The streams were A, B, C, D and Remove, 'A' being the top ability group and 'Remove' the lowest, although I have no idea of the origin of this term. I was placed in the 'D' stream. In a way this was predictable: Those of us starting school in the Autumn term were grouped and assessed along with those who had started in the previous two terms, i.e. after Easter and in January so we were, therefore, the youngest in the year group with only one term in school as opposed to two or three terms respectfully. To be categorised and 'labelled' after such a short time did seem extreme. Further, given that it was then impossible to move up a class unless you were at the very top of your current class, it was all rather unfair. This was exacerbated by the fact that unless you reached the dizzy heights of the 'B' class by the final junior school year you were not allowed to take the 11+, the benchmark in those days that could lead to a place in a grammar or secondary modern school.

During the infant years I was absent for several weeks suffering from glandular fever, and as a result subsequently missed out on two mornings a week for eighteen months in order to attend a clinic for Sun-Ray Treatment. Aside from all this I was, by all accounts, 'a late developer'.

I remember at one time sitting at my desk dreaming that I would like to become a junior schoolteacher. Some hope! But, I worked hard in those infant and junior years and against the odds did make it to that elusive 'B' stream in time for the final junior school year. Unfortunately it was only the 'A' stream pupils who were specifically groomed for the forthcoming tests so, unsurprisingly, on the first attempt I failed the scholarship (11+) exam. Having a summer birthday I was actually only ten.

Despite the struggle to 'beat the system' and make it through the 'streams' I do have many happy memories of my years in the infant and junior school.

The school I attended had infant, junior and senior sections all in one long building divided by double doors across the two long corridors that ran the whole length of the building. The Infant School was at one end and was just single storey, the Junior School was at the other end. It mirrored the Infant department being also single storey. The Senior School was in the middle and was on two levels. There were additional prefabricated buildings within the grounds and a very large playing field at the Junior School end, used mostly by the Senior School pupils. There was also a large grassed area behind the school used by the Juniors.

One of the delights in the Infant School was the annual trek to the Junior School for the Christmas concert. We all made our way, via one of the corridors, from the Infant School through the Senior School and into the Junior School. It was quite an adventure for us. But the real fun was the concert itself and the highlight, an act by the Headmaster of the Junior School and a male teacher from the Infant School. The two of them would dress up as policemen, plaster their faces in makeup, and perform the 'The Bold Gendarmes". We would laugh until the tears ran down our cheeks. There was always an encore.

This more recent photograph of the school still shows the main structure of the whole building as it was in the 1950s

The highlight of the Junior School year was the annual trip to the seaside. We would arrive at Filey when the tide was 'out' and on the wet sand we would have a sandcastle competition. In the afternoon we were allowed to roam around the shops. On the way home we would stop at a fish and chip restaurant for 'high tea'. I don't ever remember having to write about the trip the next day: It was just a fun day out, a real experience for most of us in those days when the majority of families did not own a car.

In both the Infant and the Junior School we had one class teacher with whom we stayed for most of the day. We had a visiting PE specialist in the Infant school. In the final year of the Junior School there were two afternoons in the week when the girls from two classes joined forces for sewing / handwork with the female teacher of one class whilst the boys were with the male teacher from the other class. We sometimes listened to stories or music while we worked.

Earlier I mentioned slates and slate pencils. These were still used in many schools throughout the 1950s. I have a vague recollection of using a small blackboard with chalk rather than a slate and slate pencil. Later on in the Infant School we used pencils. In the Juniors, when we began to do 'joined up' writing, we used pen and ink (i.e. pens with nibs). We sat at double desks with inkwells positioned at the right hand side. The teacher would come round the class filling the little pots, which fitted into the wells, with ink. Can you just imagine the mess?

Later on in my school life we had fountain pens and eventually pens with cartridges: a much cleaner and more efficient way of working.

A double desk with inkwells to the right:
No consideration was ever given to left-handed pupils.

The transition from the Juniors to the Seniors was a major change. Instead of struggling so hard to move up a class we, along with pupils from two other junior schools, took another exam and were re-streamed accordingly for the Senior School. I was placed in the top class out of a total of 13 classes.

The year spent in the Senior School was a complete change from anything that had gone before. In the first place, with a combined intake of pupils from three junior schools, there were many new faces. We moved around the school for lessons in different subjects taught by different teachers and were introduced to lots of new subjects. We may not have experienced the smooth transition that is seen as an ideal nowadays but a new beginning can be refreshing, leaving behind any accumulated 'baggage'. We were all on an even platform, equally matched academically with our peers in the same class. Whatever may be said about 'streaming', being correctly placed with those of a similar standard made a lot of sense. We could learn together and the teachers could focus at one level without having to cater for a whole range of ability.

However, not all aspects of this year in the Senior School were good. One of the less admirable sides was the use, or rather the abuse, of corporal punishment. I must stress here that, at the time, the use of the cane or similar was considered an acceptable form of punishment, as had been the case for many years past. But, in this school, several male teachers frequently 'lashed out' for no good reason. One occasion in particular comes to mind. Shortly after 9 a.m. on a morning during the first term, the teacher from the next classroom came to the door of our room and ordered all the boys to line up. He then made each hold out a hand and struck them with a rough block of wood. He warned that this was for doing nothing so "just wait until you do something". This to me was barbaric.

Several times our own class teacher, who also taught French, warned that if we did not learn our French verbs we would be caned. French was never my best subject and I was constantly terrified by these threats. Most of the staff, I hasten to add, were not so cruel.

Later that school year, towards the end of the spring term, those of us who wished to do so were allowed to re-sit the scholarship. This time I was successful, attaining a place at a top grammar school. I was relieved to get away from the senior school and very excited at the prospect of attending the all girls grammar school along with my 'best friend' and a number of other girls from my class. It did not disappoint and was eventually to change my life.

The grammar school was a whole new experience and one that I thoroughly enjoyed and appreciated. At the end of the fifth year I attained sufficient 'O' levels to qualify for entry to a teacher training college. Regrettably, my parents were not well off and my mother was anxious that I leave school and start work. After a short spell in an office I made a successful application to the library service where I subsequently worked for over two years, interrupted by the birth of my son and a lengthy illness. Whilst working in the library I studied for 'A' levels in English and Art.

At the age of 21, married with a young child, I finally realised my life-long ambition and began a teacher-training course. My focus was 'infants', although on completion I was qualified to teach children from nursery through to 16 years of age.

Comment:

Although initially disappointed I have no regrets at not staying on into the sixth form at school. I feel that I benefitted considerably from the experience in the work place, apart from which, I really enjoyed my time in the library. To go directly from school to college or university and straight back to school is not necessarily the best option. Having some experience of life in the 'real world' served to enrich my own life and provide an added dimension to bring to the classroom. Further, I have no regrets at being 'a slow learner' as a young child. Struggling to keep up, finding the work difficult proved an asset rather than a drawback in the teaching of young children. It gave me a clearer understanding of the problems that pupils encounter when learning proves a challenge, and I was undoubtedly better equipped to support them.

The system of 'streaming' at such an early stage was harsh and unfair, as those of us who were born in the summer term were at an obvious disadvantage. However, having a second chance at the 11+, when we were actually eleven, made up for this anomaly. Sadly, nowadays the situation is hardly any better. Despite the fact that no child is legally obliged to be in school until their fifth birthday, in England they are expected to begin formal education in the September of the year in which they will become five. This means that all pupils begin statutory education before the age of five and some have barely passed their fourth birthday. Parents who feel that their child is too young can defer to the following year, but once they do start some authorities insist that they proceed straight to the second year thus missing out on the reception year altogether. At the time of writing, this problem is being highlighted and criticized.

As a child from a working class family I was privileged, along with many of my peers, to be given the chance to attend a grammar school. Ultimately, this resulted in individuals from poorer social backgrounds entering professions and government: a real asset for the country. In closing the grammar schools in favour of massive comprehensives, opportunities for generations of working class children have been seriously jeopardized, exactly the opposite of the original intention.

CHAPTER 2
Teacher Training 1968 – 1971

In 1968 I began a three-year course at a Teacher Training College. At 21 I was regarded as a mature student. Although a few of my fellow students were married I was the only one with a young child. It was quite a challenge but also had its advantages. Much of the work in 'Education' evolved round child development and having an 18 month old provided an ideal subject for observation during the course.

We had only been in college for a few days when we were allocated the school in which we were to experience our first teaching practice during the summer term of the following year. We had an introductory week in the school and it was suggested that we could organise visits to the school on Wednesday afternoons during the year. I arranged to do this.

The school I was allocated was quite small consisting only of infant classes. The classrooms were located around the school hall. The Headmistress's office doubled as a library where the children were allowed to visit independently but be under her supervision. Before playtime each morning the Headmistress led an assembly at which the children's work was central. A fuss was always made of birthdays, with an artificial cake and candles to hand. The Headmistress knew the names of every child: There was a real warmth and genuine caring atmosphere in the school.

Following the latest trend, the morning began with art and craftwork, a host of 'messy' activities, which the children thoroughly enjoyed. It was anticipated that some of the work for the rest of the day could be inspired through these activities. It appeared to work quite well.

When the time came for the official teaching practice I was familiar with the class routine and had built up a good rapport with the children.

The pupils were very curious when my tutor from the college visited. She was a rather old-fashioned lady and was wearing gloves. They asked if she was my mother, then if she was my aunt. When I responded that she was not, one child piped up, "well, has she come to read the meter?"

As my first experience in teaching it was truly delightful. The teachers were relaxed and had the full support of the Headmistress, who knew every pupil and even took her turn on playground duty. The children themselves were encouraged and responsive in their work and appeared at ease and happy. It was an ideal learning environment.

In the second year at college we were sent out to schools in groups. We attended a half-day a week for most of a term and were expected to work as a team. It was useful to co-operate with fellow students and to share ideas.

In the third and final year we spent several weeks in one school for our final teaching practice. In my case it was a particularly awful experience. Two of us were placed in the same school. We were meant to spend the early part of the practice working under the supervision of the class teacher, and then gradually be left to handle the class on our own. The Headmistress had different ideas. She was not having *her* classes and *her* pupils left in the care of students.

The tutor from college was *a man* and 'God forbid' she was not having *a man* in her school, so she turned him away three times. He was not allowed to come in to see me. She did, however, accept a female inspector in to observe a lesson. It was the only time I was left in sole charge of the class. I was in the process of dismissing the class from a PE lesson in the hall. The children were exiting from one corner, down some steps leading to the classroom, as the Headmistress entered through a door at the opposite corner accompanied by the Inspector. In a very loud, severe voice she called the children back into the hall and scolded them for running. This was definitely not the case but I did not dare contradict her. She then left me to dismiss the class again. At this point the Inspector followed me to the classroom where I supervised the children getting changed and continued with the next lesson. I was thoroughly shaken and, clearly, that was exactly as the Headmistress intended.

On another occasion we were in the hall having dinner. One child was refusing to eat. To my horror, the Headmistress sat the boy on her knee and, forcing his head back by his hair, she physically rammed the food down his throat.

A girl in one of the classes had very supportive parents who, in a bid to assist her reading, purchased the reading scheme books. The Headmistress was furious. "How dare they?" These were *her* children, it was *her* school and no one else was going to teach them. She switched the girl onto a different reading scheme. This happened again and the Headmistress again switched the girl onto yet another alternative scheme.

I doubt that this Headmistress would have got away with any of the above nowadays. As regards the dinnertime scenario, someone would have whipped out a mobile phone and taken a photograph of the incident and that would have been the end of her career. Her whole attitude was truly appalling.

When comparing notes with my fellow student in the school it was clear that we were both equally diligent in the preparation and presentation of our lessons, so we came to the conclusion that the Headmistress had decided right from the beginning that, no matter what, one of us would 'shine' and the other, if she had her way, would fail. Being conservative in her views I believe she 'had it in for me'. I was classed as a 'mature' student although only three years older that the majority of students. Also, I was a married woman and had a child. As if that was not bad enough, I had a male tutor!

Although she fell short of failing me the Headmistress certainly had a very good try. As a student I felt vulnerable, but the whole atmosphere in the school was grim. The teachers were tense and the children afraid of the Headteacher whom I can only describe as a bully.

On returning to the college following this dreadful episode I was asked to see the Head of Education. She was most apologetic that I had been subjected to this experience and said that the college would not use the school in question again. Much later in my career I was a lecturer and tutor myself involved in the training of teachers, and looking back I had to wonder that I was not called away from the school when my tutor was 'thrown out'. In similar circumstances I would have been asking some serious questions about the merits of subjecting a student to such appalling practice. I can only imagine that this was due to a distinct shortage of placement schools in the area and the subsequent difficulties such a decision would have created.

At the time of my initial teacher training, planning was a

necessary and vital part of the procedure, as was careful preparation. However, the paperwork was manageable and limited to what was necessary.

PART 2

LIFE IN AN INNER CITY PRIMARY SCHOOL

CHAPTER 3

Baptism of Fire

Nine a.m. The first day of a new school year and for five newly qualified teachers, hovering in the corridor, a rude awakening to life in an inner city primary school is about to unfold.

It's 1971. Maybe that seems remote to the reader but it was a time of forward thinking[1], experimentation and, some might now say, pending disaster in education. Our training had in no way prepared us for the 'baptism of fire' we were about to experience.

The school we had been allocated was one that those with any knowledge of the area would be careful to avoid but, as new recruits and applicants to the education authority rather than an individual school, we had little choice. We were at least fortunate in those days in that there were jobs for all but, as the saying goes, 'beggars can't be choosers'. It was, however, shameful that such a high proportion of inexperienced young teachers should find themselves in what can at best be described as a challenging or, as will shortly become apparent, a near impossible situation.

Of the five new staff, I really believe I had drawn the short straw. The Headmistress, in her wisdom, decided that I looked the most 'motherly' and was therefore designated the youngest children. To explain, there were three 'reception' classes divided according to the age of the children. Those in the class I was allocated would turn five from December to March. Since none

---

[1] The Plowden Report published in 1967 had a significant impact on Education.

of them had had any pre-school or nursery experience, it was, for all of them, their very first day in an education establishment. Being the youngest of the intake classes it was called the 'Admission Class'. This was apparently significant as, according to the Headmistress, it meant that I was not entitled to the support of the designated Nursery Assistant because it was not called a 'Nursery' class. Besides which, the Nursery Assistant, again according to the Headmistress, was required to help the School Secretary with administrative duties. Another shameful situation!

'Induction' was not a familiar term in 1971 and neither the new staff nor the pupils were a party to this now commonplace procedure. On that first day of the new term all of the new entrants gathered in the hall, any remaining parents present were dismissed and the children were escorted to the door of their new classroom. As I opened the door of my room, the children, all 33 of them, tumbled in together, many falling over each other in a race to the very large Wendy House or the rocking horse, others totally bewildered.

How is it possible to settle 33 four year olds, with no concept of social behaviour, into some semblance of order? Did the powers that be seriously imagine that by some kind of magic so many infants, hardly more than babies, could be organised and controlled by a single adult?

So began my first day as a qualified primary school teacher.

CHAPTER 4
Setting the Scene

The School and the Catchment Area

This inner city primary school for children aged four to nine shared a campus with a middle school for pupils aged nine to 13, although in reality the two buildings were detached and quite separate, being about 100 yards apart and on different levels. The campus, as indeed the whole area, can best be described as a concrete jungle. The few trees scattered around the edge of the playground could scarcely be recognised as such, their tall trunks and sparse foliage towering so far above our heads as to render them generally unnoticed.

The estate, built between the two world wars, mostly housed families in the lowest income bracket, predominately white: In the six and a half years I taught at the school I only ever came across two children from other ethic backgrounds. There were a few children in attendance who came from private houses on the edge of the estate.

Many of the homes were in a dilapidated state of repair, often filthy with boarded up windows and neglected gardens, although possession of the latest commodities was not uncommon. Almost all of the children qualified for free school meals, a factor which eventually rendered the school an 'Education Priority Area' giving staff a supplement in salary.

The main school building was old and, until brightened with a coat of paint about half way through my time there, it was rather worn and sad. In addition to the main building there was a prefabricated unit, 'the hut', accommodating two classrooms. Within the main building was a generous hall, which served as both a gym and a dining room. There was also a library area, offices for the Secretary and the Headmistress, and two staff rooms linked by a staff toilet area. I mention this because when I first arrived at the school it was made clear that one staffroom was for the teachers of the younger children and the other for the teachers of the older classes and 'ne'er the twain shall meet', so to speak. Worse than that certain seats were 'reserved' for particular members of staff because 'they always sat there'. I am glad to report that with five new staff members and a further large turnover of staff the following year this nonsense came to an end.

All of the rooms were on one level, but there was a loft area accessed from a storeroom, which no one ever mentioned until it was abruptly brought to everyone's attention during one Christmas vacation when a criminal was found to have taken residence up there in an attempt to escape justice!

One of the children's cloakrooms occupied an open area alongside a corridor. This included three small 'infant' toilets in a row with swing doors facing the corridor. My instructions were to line my whole class up beside these toilets so that the children, both boys and girls, could 'go'. When the boys used the Wendy House in the classroom as a more convenient place to relieve themselves one cannot be too surprised!

There was a large playground outside but no grassed area. The huge iron gates were always open allowing freedom of movement for everyone. Unfortunately this made it easy for young children to 'escape', so a member of staff chasing a child around the estate was not an uncommon sight.

The Classroom

My classroom was the largest in the school occupying a corner position with a set of French doors opening out into the playground. Despite this it was a dismal room, sadly in need of a coat of paint, with shabby tables and chairs and even shabbier equipment. A very large Wendy House filled with worn out furniture and wooden bricks took up one corner of the room. The cupboards were jam packed with an array of games and jigsaw puzzles: The latter mostly had pieces missing and nothing was new or even remotely so. There was also a rocking horse, a piano (unfortunately I cannot play) and a wire book rack attached to the back of a cupboard to create a book corner.

The classroom floor was just bare wooden boards with gaps between, in places wide enough for little fingers to penetrate and, as will be described later, through which many an object could be deposited and lost forever.

Bare wooden floorboards with gaps in between

In order to enhance the learning process and also to show off the children's work the large expanse of wall space in most rooms was covered from floor to ceiling with sugar paper on which charts, displays and the pupils' efforts could be mounted. In many instances I found this excessive. However, after years of using staple guns and blue tack to attach all this paraphernalia to the walls, they were in such a mess that to leave any inch of them bare was simply not a feasible option. Attractive and purposeful charts and displays etc. are a real asset in any primary classroom but what young child is going to take notice of a supposed teaching aid placed just inches from the roof of a high ceilinged classroom? The gaps in the floorboards are much more interesting! Aside from that, since when did clambering up a ladder and performing the antics involved in manoeuvering paper and a staple gun at that height become part of a teacher's remit?

The lack of decent games and toys to occupy up to 37 four year olds (the number of children eventually assigned to my class) was indeed depressing. But, as if this was not bad enough, books were equally sparse and there were no workbooks or worksheets. Photocopiers, as yet, did not feature in any school, so work cards covered with clear vinyl had to be produced by each individual teacher. Reading books for the main school reading scheme *were* available but we were to pilot a new approach called 'Breakthrough to Literacy' and that was another story - more to follow.

There was no running water in the classroom.

The School Day

In my first year the school day ran from 8.55 a.m. until 3.55

p.m. with a one and a half hour lunch break and morning and afternoon playtime breaks. As teachers of infants and juniors we taught all subjects and had no free time. In addition, we were expected to supervise our classes having dinner, which with very young children could take well over an hour. We also took turns, a week at a time, to do playground duty during the morning and afternoon breaks. 'Dinner ladies' patrolled the playground at lunchtime but there was no such assistance for the playtime breaks.

In future years the infants and juniors (i.e. the Primary School or First School) finished at 3.30 p.m. but this was of little consolation since many had to wait to be collected by older siblings and had, meantime, to be supervised by their class teachers.

The Curriculum

On first arriving at the school I was presented with a booklet outlining the curriculum for the Admission Class. This set of guidelines was clearly years out of date and totally inappropriate: It was obvious that no one had checked it for a very long time. When challenging its content, i.e. asking the Headmistress where I might find 37 'beds' on which the children were to lie down for their afternoon nap, I was simply 'waved off'. (This piece of fiction had obviously been created for a group of toddlers.) It was reiterated that my class was an admission class and that as such I was not entitled to a nursery assistant. Furthermore, and again because it was *called* the 'Admission Class', the pupils would be expected to be able to read and write by the end of the school year.

As I recall, these guidelines were never replaced and no

further guidance was ever forthcoming.

So what was the curriculum?

Reading, Writing and Arithmetic; Religious Education; Art and Craft; Physical Education and Music.

This all sounds fairly logical and as a trained teacher it was assumed that I had all the knowledge and expertise necessary to fulfill this 'simple' task. But, stop for a moment and consider the implications. There was no support and little in the way of appropriate teaching aids. Children who cannot read and have no experience of following instructions cannot be left to their own devices, they cannot 'get on with the work', and everything has to be 'spoon fed'. Having little or no concept of social skills, they have no idea of what is acceptable behaviour and what is not, they have to experience social interaction, they have to be told when their actions cannot be tolerated. A myriad of skills needed to be taught before any formal teaching could even begin. These children, as will become more apparent in the following chapters, were simply not ready for formal education and I was not ready for them. I thought then, as I still think now, that one adult faced with 37 four year olds, as described above, cannot cater satisfactorily for all their needs.

Teachers of the youngest children had little, if any marking, but in terms of workload this was weighted by preparation. Apart from reading scheme books, all materials had to be produced in the form of work cards, an ongoing process taking up hours of time each evening. In addition, classrooms were required to be made appealing, surrounded by learning aids as well as attractive displays to show off children's work and give encouragement. Conjuring up ideas to inspire young minds was always on the agenda.

Often people comment on teachers' supposed short working hours but do they realise the amount of work involved at either end of the official school day?

The Admission Class

The children assigned to my class turned five between Christmas and Easter, meaning that as they started school in September many were scarcely four and a half years old. A survey carried out in this area at this time by an expert in the field of language development revealed that, on average, these children were 18 months behind 'the norm'. From my personal experience in this school I would say this was indeed the case. There were, of course, a few exceptions, individuals who were at least average in their speech development but, on the whole, I would have to agree that the results of the survey were not far from the truth. In fact, almost one third of the pupils, when eventually assessed at the age of seven, were found to fall into the category of the 'Educational Subnormal'. These children were eventually allocated places in an ESN School. (A school for the Educationally Subnormal: i.e. for those who were deemed too poor to cope with learning in mainstream.) This terminology would be frowned upon today but I am simply relaying the facts as they were at that time. Nowadays such children as these would be allocated learning support within the mainstream school. For children under the age of seven neither of these options was available, so class teachers were just expected to manage.

In the classroom the tables were arranged to accommodate groups of up to eight children. It was usual to assign the name of a colour to each of these tables and eventually, though not initially, each colour would come to represent a reading ability group. This system supposedly disguised such information from the pupils themselves, although in reality most were well aware of where they slotted in.

Being responsible for the same class for the entire time and, for the most part in the one room, the day had to be divided to provide a variety of experiences for the children and different teaching methods employed. Education during this period was moving away from class teaching and emphasis was focused on groups and individuals. Buzzwords and phrases such as 'child centred' and 'catering for individual needs' were becoming fashionable. Rote learning was 'out' including the chanting of 'multiplication tables' as was 'phonics'. Although the latter was later to figure highly once again as it had in the past.

In the post war years when a shortage of qualified teachers combined with the 'baby boom' resulted in large classes, often of 50 or more, whole class teaching was the only feasible approach. As class sizes were reduced group teaching became the more acceptable strategy and class teaching was often frowned upon. Personally I don't believe that it is possible for one teacher to cater successfully for several different groups at the same time, especially when the children involved cannot read or write and have little or no experience of social interaction. I would suggest that classes, even of 30, are still too large for this to work effectively; whilst concentrating on one group, what *are* the other groups doing?

Certain activities have been described by 'educationalists' as 'bum stickers', activities designed by teachers who are supposedly too lazy to keep each of their charges purposefully occupied at all times. It doesn't take a genius to work out the unfairness of this criticism. It also highlights how removed from reality those who pontificate about education can be.

Obviously, I had to find the best possible strategies to cope in such a situation, and do the best I could to support these very young children. A fairly regular routine needed to be employed to help them not only feel secure but also give variety and interest to the day. I attempted to achieve this by:
- Bringing the whole class together at regular intervals to share their news, draw attention to objects and displays around the room, sing songs, learn nursery rhymes and number rhymes and listen to stories;
- Giving opportunities for both social and language development through play;
- Providing 'educational' games, puzzles and construction toys;
- Introducing different tactile experiences through art and craftwork.

'Messy' activities are a delight for young children, but with no running water in the classroom and cleaners who expected the classroom to be left clean for them, providing these activities was a real challenge. After one member of the cleaning staff complained to the Headmistress when I'd dared to have children working with clay, I was told that I must take the whole class into the corridor and leave them there whilst I sweep the floor and wipe the tables myself. I'm not a 'messy' person by nature and would always encourage my pupils to tidy up as best they could, but this situation was quite ridiculous.

Making provision for the children to paint was a real nightmare. I had to carry a bucket of water from the nearest staff room along the corridor to the classroom in order to mix paint, wash brushes and deal with the inevitable mess. The children had to be trusted to go along to the infant toilets to wash their hands. When it was the turn of my class to have the shared water tray for the purpose of water play it was an even greater headache.

Physical Education also proved difficult, basically through lack of facilities: access to the gym was limited as the room doubled as a dining area and was used by every class. There were no playing fields.

Having described in brief the catchment area, the school and the curriculum and outlined some of the difficulties, now for the real 'fun and games'.

CHAPTER 5
The Children

Something To Think About

Before I embark on sharing some of the many incidents - amusing; tragic; heartrending; bizarre - I would like to say that, though incredibly challenging and at times impossible, these children were, overall, a delight. Although their behaviour may on the surface be construed as 'naughty', I really believe that this was not usually the case. On arrival to the 'Admission Class' many had little or no social skills and no concept of how to behave in a class or group situation. I don't suppose many of them had ever had to sit down at a table or listen to instructions and they had never had to 'line up'. Many did not know how to use a pencil, how to put on their coat or shoes, how to use a knife and fork. They were bewildered; frightened; excited; curious and much more. They were four years old (but many scarcely three in terms of their speech and language development), thrown into an unfamiliar environment and having to share the attention of a single adult with over 30 other children.

How would you behave?

Our Lives In Their Hands

Maybe this appears to be back to front, surely it should be their lives in our hands and, of course, that is true. But the above statement is also true, for teaching is not necessarily the safest occupation and this applies to primary as well as secondary schools, although perhaps not quite in the same way or to the same degree.

Even very young children can display enormous strength

when angry or frustrated and some of the language from a four year old in this school could 'turn the air blue'. I have been kicked and sworn at by children 'having a tantrum'. On one occasion I was 'attacked' by a child charging full force towards me with a chair (more of that later). I have been accidentally showered in paint.

Angry parents can be a real force to be reckoned with. At one point I was given strict instructions by the Headmistress to avoid insisting a particular child do any work. His father had attacked the teacher of a sibling in the middle school with a knife: A court case was pending.

Following an incident where a child had been involved in an accident in the classroom the irate mother came into school complaining to the Headmistress that I was responsible. When I explained exactly what had happened she was, fortunately, pacified. On another occasion a child told her parents that during the course of a school day I had taken her to hospital and 'undressed' her. As it happened, I was away from school that day so I was 'off the hook'. This latter incident indicates just how easy it is for a child to make a false accusation against a teacher and, when one considers that this was a five year old, the implications with much older children are horrendous, placing an innocent teacher's reputation and livelihood on the line.

A particularly dreadful incident occurred when a child was excluded from school because she was found to have head lice. The child was sent home at lunchtime with a note giving instructions not to return until her head was clean. The father stormed into the school, burst into the Headmistress's office and hauled her by the hair up and over her desk. She was left badly bruised with a significant bald patch.

Apart from violence we were also at risk from 'sniffs, sneezes and diseases'. This applied especially to newly qualified teachers. Normal coughs, colds and flu viruses are rife amongst young children and easily passed on in a crowded classroom. Those teachers who had escaped some of the common childhood ailments as youngsters themselves would often succumb once they started teaching. In my case I was particularly unlucky. Just six weeks into my first year I was diagnosed with Infective Hepatitis, contracted from one of the pupils in my class. At this point the Nursery Assistant, who had been banned from assisting me, was brought in to take the class. After three weeks, she was signed off sick. A supply teacher was then appointed but he only managed one day. He was overwhelmed by this unruly class and just could not cope! Unfortunately, a few weeks later we learned that he too had contracted Hepatitis: he became so ill that he was signed off for a total of six months.

The Class

The class I had been allocated was extremely difficult to manage, in fact 'impossible' would probably be a more accurate term. Mid-way through the course of the year the Deputy Headteacher, a very understanding and caring person, commented that the last teacher to be faced with such a difficult class had 'walked out' and never taught again. Not perhaps the most helpful remark but it was kindly meant as an expression of sympathy. In my situation, having invested so much time and effort into training for the profession, I had no intention of giving up.

It would be easy to say that it was the children who made life difficult but, in reality, as individuals they were a delight.

They just needed time: time to adapt; time to learn how to cope in a social situation. They needed *my* time, but with upwards of 30 pupils in the class, I did not have enough time to give them, either as individuals or in small groups. They needed to be adequately cared and catered for before any formal teaching could take place and this was simply not possible without adequate staffing.

I have heard people say some of the silliest things about teaching young children:

"It is just baby-sitting."

(Whoever would consider giving a baby-sitter over thirty children to care for?)

"They don't take up much space so you can fit more of them into a classroom."

(How can anyone think that a young child needs less space than an older one, and consequently have a less favourable pupil / teacher ratio?)

"It's OK to take them off on holiday during term time, because primary education isn't that important." What nonsense!

Worryingly these statements don't just come from lay people, they come from educationalists. It puzzled me how an education authority could stipulate that a practical class in a secondary school must have no more than 20 pupils, whereas primary classes could have a maximum of 33. So much primary education is of a practical nature that this attitude defies belief. As the foundation for future learning surely more consideration needed to be given to the staffing arrangements in our primary schools.

In this inner city school there was never a real problem with parents taking children out of school on holiday since most didn't go away on holiday and many rarely ventured from the estate.

However, absenteeism *was* a problem. After the first morning, when 33 children arrived at the same time, there was rarely the same number of children in attendance for two consecutive sessions. Even on that first day one child did not return in the afternoon. It was not until later that I discovered the girl in question had actually played truant. Her mother had collected her at the end of the morning and either sent her on her own for the afternoon or else not waited to see her safely into the school building.

This kind of erratic attendance adds to the frustrations of a teacher's job. By the end of the term my register looked like a giant game of noughts and crosses!

The children, having made their entrance into the classroom, - now what? One of the most important tasks for the class teacher is to learn the names of the children as quickly as possible. This is essential to gain their confidence and establish some form of discipline. Prior to the start of the term I made sure I was familiar with all the names from the register and had made labels for tables and coat pegs. Now I needed to link the names to the faces. As you might imagine this was more easily said than done. Four year olds are not programmed to stay in one place and concentrate for very long. For several days chaos reigned. There was crying, temper tantrums, fights and a few 'accidents'. For this latter eventuality there was access to a collection of spare pants but no assistance to attend to a child in this predicament. Often there was no option but to escort the whole class to the three infant toilets: what a nightmare! Despite everything, over time a daily routine was established and at least some of the children began to settle.

Many of these youngsters were clearly 'disturbed'. There was evidence of abuse although physical signs are not always easy to detect and emotional problems not easy to deal with. One child screamed frequently throughout the entire first term, many others would, at times, be clearly distressed, inconsolable and unable to articulate their problems.

One little boy was 'sewn in for the winter'. This was a phenomenon totally unfamiliar to me. In this case his vest and jumper were sewn up so that he could not undress, thereby ensuring he would stay warm during the coldest months. On the part of the parents it was an act of caring rather than neglect but, admittedly, it did not seem that way. Other children were inadequately clad. One girl shared a pair of knickers with an older sister and her mother: they took it in turns, day about, to wear the precious item. I realise this 'beggars belief' but it is absolutely true.

Some children seemed to thrive in the face of adversity.

On a Monday morning, early in the first term, one of the boys came rushing excitedly into the classroom. He was desperate to relay his weekend news:

"Guess what, my dad's in prison".

On another occasion, later in the school year, another boy wrote about his visit to the seaside the previous Saturday. The highlight of the trip was accompanying his uncle into the local 'Woolworth' store for the sole purpose of shoplifting. He even told what they 'got away with'.

One of the girls in the class was the youngest child of an elderly, sick mother whose ailments included epilepsy. The older siblings were grown up and away from home and Ann was frequently left alone to look after her mother. Ann was a really lovely child: she would sometimes come and sit beside me and talk about the ways in which she helped at home. She was like a little old lady herself, so mature for such a small child and 'old-fashioned': it was like speaking adult to adult. She took her responsibilities very seriously. What an enormous burden to be borne on such young shoulders.

Head lice was a constant plague and the 'Nit Nurse', as she was rather unfortunately nicknamed, was a regular presence in the school. It is said that lice prefer clean heads, so no matter the school or the area the problem exists. However, in this school the ignorance and unwillingness of some parents to address the problem thoroughly meant that it never went away. Several of the teachers, especially those of us with long hair, were always at risk of becoming infected, so the nurse regularly checked our heads as well.

Individuals

Darren

Darren was an 'unfortunate' child in many ways. With one leg slightly shorter than the other and being constantly drugged up with phenobarbitone to control his epilepsy, he had difficulty walking from one side of the classroom to the other without falling over. Although not physically attractive he was a pleasant natured little boy and thereby rather likeable. He did not appear to be particularly talented in any way and, for the most part, showed little academic ability. However, one day whilst I was attending to a group of children reading, he joined the circle around my desk. As he was not being disruptive, I did not send him away. To my amazement, as one child 'stumbled' over the words, Darren began to read them fluently from his vantage point, i.e. upside down. He was obviously curious and by listening to and observing the other children he had been absorbing rather more information than he had previously let on.

One of the facts about young children's learning is that they will often have 'spurts' when, for a period of time, they will advance very quickly. A 'secret' in the primary classroom is to 'grab' them when this happens and move them on as fast as possible. I never had a problem moving pupils to a higher reading group as and when they were able to cope.

Although Darren made progress he was never going to be the smartest in the class. I was, however, rather taken aback when the Headmistress indicated that he was destined for a school for the 'educationally subnormal', the sole reason being that his older brother was already there. I really was horrified that such an assumption could be made.

Julia

Julia was a small, rather vacant child from a very poor family background. She had two older brothers, the elder of whom had already been assessed as ESN and would shortly be transferred to a special school. According to one of the other teachers, when the mother first brought him to school to be registered he was in a pram. Apparently, she had not realised that babies, as they grow, need to be taken out of their prams.

Often Julia would turn up for school in the morning eating what seemingly constituted her breakfast: The dregs left in the bottom of a packet of cornflakes or, on one occasion, an almost empty jar of salad cream.

Julia was frequently very poorly clad, wearing, for instance, a short-sleeved cotton frock in the middle of winter and having no coat. A member of staff, who had a daughter the same age though rather taller, brought in some clothes for Julia. She asked the mother if she would like these things. The mother appeared delighted and Julia left school that day wearing a lovely warm coat. However, the following morning she arrived at school minus the coat. When asked what had happened to it the mother replied, "I didn't like her in it."

One day, at lunchtime, I was walking along the corridor beside the infant cloakroom and the three small toilets that faced outwards, as previously described. Suddenly, a voice called out to me. I turned to see the door of one of the toilets swing open and Julia's mother sitting on the toilet waving her arms and shouting to me to look at her.

You couldn't make it up!

Karen

With many years experience teaching all stages of primary school children I have to say that, in general, it was the boys who would cause the most trouble. The primary school teacher would often dread a class with an imbalance of boys and girls where boys were in the majority. However, I would have to add to this the fact that a difficult girl could be much harder to deal with than any number of boys. This was certainly true of Karen.

A small, delicate child with the cutest little face, she appeared the picture of innocence. She was, however, wild and, for much of the time, totally out of control. Every day for most of the first term she screamed: It was relentless.

Despite her small stature she fought with every child in the class, biting, kicking, pinching and thumping. On one occasion at the end of the lunchtime break, as the children were coming into the classroom via the French doors, she tripped and fell at the threshold. The other children proceeded to trample over her on their way in, ignoring her screams - poetic justice maybe.

When a relief teacher took over my class for a day whilst I was off sick, being exasperated by this unruly child, he hauled her away along the corridor under his arm as she kicked and screamed. Meantime, the school secretary was on the telephone to the secretary of the middle school: Staff in that building reportedly heard Karen's screams.

One day as some children were entering the room Karen dashed like lightning across the room and caught her little finger in the door. This time her screams were 'for real'. The tiny finger was hanging on by a thread. Holding the finger in place I raced down the corridor with her, tears in my eyes, to the school office. An ambulance was called and she was rushed into hospital. Thankfully the finger was saved.

Karen could dart from one side of the room to the other in a flash, knocking down any obstacles in her path. On one occasion another child had climbed into a doll's pram. Karen took the pram and ran with it full force right into a cupboard. Another time she picked up a chair and, with the four legs pointed outwards away from her, she made a beeline straight for me. The strength behind small children should never be underestimated!

Many of her antics were so dangerous that I often used to fear that she would never live to adulthood. Sadly, how right I was. At the age of ten she was killed as she played 'chicken' on the road. Hers was the first funeral I ever attended and it was so tragic to see the tiny coffin.

As may be deduced from the above descriptions the

problems in this school and particularly in the Admission Class were immense. Apart from teaching we were essentially social workers, for what child can begin to learn with such troubles?

Miraculously, despite everything, many of the children made remarkable progress in the basic skills during that first year.

Children's Behaviour

Rainy Days, Playtime And Food

The weather can have a profound influence on children's behaviour. When the wind whistles around the school, the children can be equally wild within. The rain has a similar effect and when children are cooped up inside all day they are invariably unsettled. Clearing aside the tables and chairs is quite a performance but on wet days it is essential to allow some freedom of movement, basically to make space for a PE lesson in the classroom. It is a well-researched fact that academic performance is enhanced when interspersed with physical activity. To deny children time to 'let off steam' is counterproductive in terms of their education.

During the actual playtimes and lunch-breaks, when children were confined to the classroom, activities were limited, usually to reading and drawing. Each teacher would have a 'rainy day box' in the classroom, often containing comics that children would bring from home. I recall an incident when a boy from another class, who had a sister in my class, came into my room with a pile of magazines for my rainy day box. Since he knew where the box was kept and I was busy, I paid little attention and simply indicated for him to go ahead and place the items in the box. It wasn't until the next wet playtime that I realised, to my horror, that some of these magazines were in fact pornographic.

Coming from low-income families, the majority of pupils were entitled to free school meals. This meant that they had at least one decent meal a day. In the 1970s, as in previous decades, school meals provided a well balanced diet. No junk food, no choice and, if I may be so bold, no nonsense. Maybe that sounds harsh by today's standards but it actually worked well. In addition, every child was entitled to one third of a pint of milk per day.

As early as 1906 milk was identified as one of the foods that could alleviate poor nutrition, considered one of the principal hindrances to learning. Following the Second World War Parliament passed the 1946 Free Milk Act. This provided free milk to all schoolchildren. Each pupil under the age of 18 was entitled to a third of a pint a day. Margaret Thatcher most famously hastened the demise of free milk in schools, although to be fair it was already in decline before she came to power.

Nowadays it is understood that the consumption of junk foods, including sugary drinks, has an adverse effect on children's behaviour and can exacerbate symptoms of ADHD[2], ultimately causing them to create havoc in the classroom.

Although the families on this estate were considered sufficiently lacking in finances that their offspring were entitled to free school meals (a blessing as indicated above), there always seemed to be enough cash for them to visit the 'Tuck Shop' before going home.

Imagine how much more challenging the behaviour of these children might have been had they been subjected to the amount

---

[2] Attention Deficit Hyperactivity Disorder

of junk foods available to children today.

Have we learned nothing over the years?

SCHOOL MILK

SCHOOL MILK CRATES

Free school milk was available for all pupils, the allocation being 1/3 pint. The bottles arrived in crates deposited in the school playground. They would be distributed to the classrooms in time for the morning break.

CHAPTER 6
The Basic Skills

Teach Them To Read And Write.

The main priority according to the Headmistress was to teach the children to read and write and, of course, this has to be the ultimate goal of any primary school. But, as is obvious, many of the children placed in the Admission Class were simply not ready. When, immediately after the Christmas holidays most were not on a reading book, questions were asked. But these pupils, with no pre-school experience, were yet to turn five, so why the panic? As a young teacher I was made to feel inadequate, as if I was unable to match up to the job. Even at the time I felt this was unjustified. I was being asked to do the impossible and, looking back, I was right! After 30 years experience in the profession I could not meet these expectations.

Thankfully, in the intervening years, nursery education has become a standard throughout the country and classroom assistance is accepted as the norm to ease the burden of teachers and allow them to do the job for which they were trained.

Breakthrough To Literacy

During my first year as a teacher a new approach to the teaching of reading was introduced for which we were a 'pilot' school. It was called 'Breakthrough to Literacy' and was based on the language experiences of the children. The materials included a three-part free standing 'slotted' folder called a 'sentence maker' for each child and a plastic stand; a large corresponding sentence maker and stand for the teacher to use for demonstration and instruction and a Breakthrough word bank, a collection of all the words, printed separately on individual pieces of laminated card and arranged on two very large 'slotted' display boards corresponding to the pages in the child's own sentence maker.

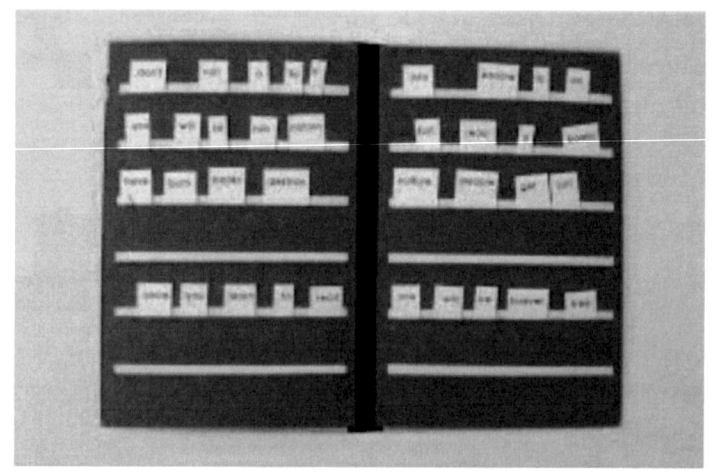

The Sentence Maker

The first two pages of the sentence maker showed words most commonly used by children in their writing. When a child wanted one of these words they would collect the word from the Breakthrough word bank: Once the word was part of the child's sight vocabulary the child was allowed to keep the word, placing it in their own folder for further use. These small word cards slotted into position in front of the corresponding word printed in the sentence maker. Each word therefore had its own set place in the sentence maker and a corresponding place in the class word bank thus allowing for ease of reference. As the child collected the words needed to make a sentence they placed them on their plastic stand. When a child required a word not found in the word bank the teacher would write the word on a separate piece of card. Such words could be stored on the third page of the sentence maker, which was blank.

So, in this way, each child would choose words to place in their stand in order to build their sentences, which would be approved / discussed with the teacher. They would then read their sentences (referred to as 'stories') back to the teacher who would write them into a book leaving a space beneath so that the child could copy them out. Alternate pages or areas of a page would be left blank for the child to add their own illustration. This would become the child's individual reading book. A great idea!

This approach required massive input from the teacher who was, in reality, expected to produce each child's reading book. Used with small numbers of children this could be very successful; it was meaningful in that the book consisted of the child's own stories and they could readily recall what they had written but, in a large class with no additional support, it proved a logistical nightmare. Remember, the gaps between the floorboards? Just guess where lots of the words on the very small pieces of card ended up.

Another instruction 'from above' was that the teacher should hear each individual child read every day. Just whom did they think they were kidding?

Alongside the more formal work, much of the skills' practice that should have been a precursor *was* going on. There were educational puzzles, opportunities for play with some monitoring and teacher intervention and a class book corner. For the last half hour of every school day I read to the class. Sometimes it was said that a teacher should tell rather than read stories to the children. That is all very well and has its place but the language of books differs from the spoken word and, in order for children to read, it is advantageous that they become familiar with this different style.

Regarding the teaching of young children, language and reading development have always been a particular interest of mine. It is fascinating that children actually learn to read and write at all for, to my mind, it is not a simple process, it does not normally 'just happen'. This is why pre-reading and pre-writing skills are so important. Children can learn so much through play and social interaction and, with thoughtful adult direction many of the necessary requirements for their development in reading and language can be acquired quite naturally. Listening and talking are essential prerequisites, for how else can they make sense of the written word? It is one of the reasons pre-school nurseries have become so important over the years. Of course, many children do have very rich experiences in the home, but for those denied this privilege, where access to books and other suitable materials has been limited and adult guidance lacking, the pre-school nursery experience has become a crucial stage in the learning process. It is a mistake and potentially damaging to plunge children into 'formal education' without providing them with the 'building blocks' needed to acquire the necessary skills in order to cope. After all, you would never expect anyone to make a cake without providing them with the basic ingredients!

Maths

Basic number work did not represent quite the same headache as dealing with reading and writing and, left to my own devices, I was able to support the children's learning in this area quite successfully. Every day, after the morning break the children would come together for number rhymes, songs and a bit of 'drama'. It was a 'fun' time with the whole class, encouraging number language as well as counting practice, with lots of repetition. In addition to this many other activities, including art and craft work, construction toys and puzzles, and an array of counting aids such as coloured beads, counters and bricks helped promote mathematical skills in one way or another. Later in the year work cards were introduced, all made up as required as no commercially produced cards or workbooks were available in the school.

CHAPTER 7
The First Year Draws to a Close

Despite the traumas of everyday life in the classroom, the experience as a whole was not all negative. We were a very close-knit staff and looking back I believe that this had a good deal to do with the challenges we faced on a daily basis. Each and every day there were tales to tell, anecdotes to share, all of which helped cement friendships amongst us. When anxious about a situation there was always a listening ear, and because we were all 'in the same boat', there was mutual understanding. In the staffroom we laughed a lot, a relief from all the trials and tribulations.

As the year progressed there were some improvements. I was able to order some new equipment including construction toys, games and puzzles as well as some new books for the class book corner. The 'Breakthrough to Literacy' materials, though a nightmare in many respects, did provide some added interest. The room was further enhanced with new furniture: desks, chairs and units to accommodate tote trays. However, ironically much of this expense was afforded by the Education Authority for the purpose of a new 'Nursery Class' to be opened for the next school session beginning in September. It would accommodate the youngest and most vulnerable children of that year's intake and be limited to 30. Thus, having struggled against all odds for an entire year, in the years that followed many children in the same age range would have the benefit of a qualified nursery teacher and three qualified nursery nurses. Furthermore this would be a designated Pre-school Nursery and there would be no pressure to begin formal teaching.

So, as the first year drew to a close the five newly qualified teachers, now one year older and a good deal wiser were to face the HMI (Her Majesty's Inspectorate). Having completed our Probationary Year we were to be informed whether or not we had been successful.

The five of us, in fear and trepidation, were huddled in a circle in the school hall. A rather tall, sophisticated gentleman entered and thence followed a short scene I will never forget. He looked around the group, eying us up one by one and, after a momentary pause, announced:

"Well, you're all still here and you're all still standing. You have survived. You've passed".

The relief was palpable!

So ended the first year.

CHAPTER 8
A New School Year

Towards the end of the first year the staff were informed as to class allocations for the following year. I was given a choice: either to take the same class into their second year or else begin again with a new intake! Working on the premise, 'better the devil you know' I decided to continue with my current class. In retrospect this was probably the wrong decision as no other class in my entire career was ever as challenging as this one and furthermore, I was unaware of what was to come.

During the summer term another girl had joined the admission class, another girl who cried and screamed incessantly. This situation created mayhem. It upset a class that had, to some extent, finally settled. Into the second year and an incident occurred that indicated this child was most likely from a very rough, potentially dangerous family background.

One morning she came into class complaining of a sore head. She was blessed with a mass of curly, dark brown hair, albeit rather unruly, which was disguising the real problem. I took it that she had a headache and, as I was unable to administer any medication, I simply offered a sympathetic ear and an assurance that it would probably soon be better. However, after she complained two or three more times I investigated further to discover that this was no ordinary headache: she had an enormous gash in the top of her head, several centimetres long and a couple of centimetres wide. When asked how it had happened she responded,

"mi dad 'it me wi' t brush". I was horrified!

I escorted her to the school office, an emergency call was made and the child was taken to hospital for investigation. It was too late for the wound to be stitched so, as far as I am aware, it was cleaned and left to heal itself. The girl returned to school and, to my knowledge, no further action was taken.

Hazards from Outwith

Not all of the problems encountered in the school stemmed from within the classroom. Incidents would frequently occur that were beyond our control but which could have a profound effect on the smooth running of the day:

During the 1970s the IRA, who were active in Northern Ireland at the time, extended their campaign to mainland Britain attacking both military and civilian targets. As a result of this, 'bomb scares' were a common occurrence throughout the country, although many would turn out to be hoaxes.

Several bomb scares, in the form of anonymous telephone calls, were made to the school, which of course, always had to be taken seriously. Normal fire practices would take place at least once each term when, generally, teachers would know that it was just 'a practice', but bomb scares were different, any one of them could be the 'real thing'. The whole school had to be evacuated and the building thoroughly searched. As with a normal fire practice the classes congregated in a designated area of the playground, but instead of returning to our classrooms within a few minutes, we had to escort the children to a nearby church where we would 'sit it out' until the potential danger was over and the 'all clear' given. As you might imagine, this was quite a performance.

One wet day some parents from nearby houses gathered at

the school gate when they saw the children assembled in the playground. A barrage of abuse was hurled at the teachers as to why their offspring were not wearing their coats. The fact that we were facing the possibility of a destructive weapon having been planted somewhere in the school and threatening the lives of us all in no way pacified them.

One afternoon whilst I was reading to the children, a rumpus began in the playground just outside my classroom window. Two mothers of children in my class were involved in a 'set to'. Screaming and shouting penetrated the room and the opponents were quite literally 'tearing each others hair out'. With the best will in the world it is impossible to maintain the full attention of a class when parents are behaving in such a violent manner just a few feet away and within sight of the children. I left the class to call for help and the police were subsequently informed.

Following a weekend it was not unusual to return to a classroom that was showered in glass from broken windows: Vandalism was rife on the estate. The consequences of this were disruptive to say the least. The whole class would have to be moved to a vacant room, usually the gym or the library, until all fragments of glass were cleared. After one such week-end I returned to discover a broken pane of glass in the French doors through which live matches had been thrown setting fire to some items in a 'dressing up' box. Fortunately, the fire had not spread: it was a miracle that the whole room had not gone up in flames.

Another hazard was packs of stray dogs. They would roam the estate and congregate in the playground. Sometimes, before the start of the school day, they would find their way into the school itself. I, together with several of my colleagues, was terrified. We would make a dash for the nearest classroom and lock ourselves in. The school secretary, a small but robust woman, would inevitably "tut-tut", chase the offending animals out of the building and call the dogcatchers.

The Real Challenge Of Year Two:
Charlie

When I agreed to take this exceptionally difficult class for a further year, rather than face a new intake of pupils, I could never have imagined what was in store.

Arguably the greatest challenge of my entire career joined the class in the form of a boy called Charlie. He was a delightful looking little boy with a twinkle in his eye and a smile to melt the hardest of hearts, but he was truly impossible.

How anyone could think that a class teacher with almost 40 pupils and no additional assistance could accommodate this child is beyond my comprehension. In later years, as a Headteacher myself, I would never have expected any member of staff to cope with such a child.

Charlie was six years old: several months older than any other child in the class. He had been held back from starting school along with other children of his own age because he was not toilet trained. However, at six, and still in nappies, with a vocabulary of only around six words, some 'genius' thought it was time he was in school and saw fit to place him in my class rather than with his own peer group.

I refused, categorically, to change his nappies, because I knew it was not possible for me to do this and maintain responsibility for the rest of the class as well. When his nappy needed changing I took him into the nursery and, either one of the nursery nurses would take him home or the school secretary would summon the assistance of an older sibling from the middle school to undertake this task. Charlie's family, as most families on the estate, did not have access to a telephone so there was no means of direct contact to ask his mother to come to collect him.

There was no way that Charlie could learn alongside any of the other children. His speech had not developed beyond that of a baby. He had no attention span and could not be still. He would dart around the room screeching and leaping onto the chairs and the tables. He would fling his arms around knocking over any objects in his path and disturbing the rest of the class. As far as control was concerned he was totally 'off the radar'.

Although at this time corporal punishment was considered acceptable in schools it was a measure I could not possibly engage in with this child. There was something seriously wrong with him: he was not simply a naughty boy. He needed the kind of specialised support in which I was not trained, and even if I had had such expertise it still would not have been possible for me to cater for him in a class situation.

On several occasions I approached the Headmistress but she refused to listen: as far as she was concerned it was not her problem. I pleaded with her, but to no avail. She would sit in her office the entire day rarely venturing out to assess what was happening in the school. From a positive point of view she never bothered the teachers: we were just 'left to get on with it'. But in a situation like this we needed support and she simply did not want to know.

Charlie's mother appeared to me a reasonable enough person. She came across as quite pleasant and showed obvious concern for her son. She was aware that there was a serious problem and during that first term made a point of approaching me to discuss the matter. I spoke with the Headmistress yet again but still without success. She revealed that Charlie was child number ten in the family and that child number nine had died: the implication being that this tragedy had occurred through neglect. She was therefore not prepared to 'entertain' the mother at all and made it clear that any form of communication with her was 'taboo'.

When the mother subsequently attended a parents' evening mid-way through the school year I explained that I was unable to seek any additional help for Charlie in my capacity as his class teacher. But, being aware that a health visitor was involved with the family, I suggested to the mother that she reiterate her concerns regarding Charlie's education to this person with a view to having him assessed. She did, in fact, take on board my advice, but things moved very slowly.

One day during the summer term I was summoned to the Headmistress's office. She was furious. Sitting behind her huge, completely empty desk she raged about the amount of work she had to do, then proceeded to thump on the desk with her fist repeating the following mantra over and over again emphasising each word or part word as a rhythm.

"You … Have … Contra … Vened … The … Education … Act".

I honestly did not know what she was talking about. Even as she calmed down sufficiently to explain, I remained baffled.

She accused me of going to the Local Education Authority behind her back and telling tales in an effort to seek some help for Charlie. None of this was true, of course. Eventually it began to dawn on me: Charlie's mother had spoken with the Health Visitor who had, in turn, approached the Department of Education.

I admitted that I had talked to the mother. Another explosion! I had no business whatever to do such a thing. This was 'a parent from Hell'. How dare I approach her when I had been specifically told not to do so.

I argued that I had not approached the mother, but the mother had come to see me on Parents' Evening, as was her right. (So few parents of children at this school were sufficiently interested to attend such evenings that appointments were never made. Those who did appear would normally see their child's class teacher straight away and, if they did have to wait, it was never for very long.)

Still fuming, but losing the battle, the Headmistress managed to inform me that an educational psychologist would be coming into the school to assess Charlie's behaviour. I should have been relieved at this information but I was in total shock. It was made clear to me during this 'interrogation' that I had 'overstepped the mark'. As a result of my actions my career was 'on the line' because, she repeated,

"You … Have … Contra … Vened … The … Education … Act".

This incident constituted one of the worst moments in my career. Having struggled with Charlie for almost a year, whilst at the same time attempting to maintain some semblance of order in the classroom and support the other pupils, I was exhausted. I could not have done any more in my capacity as a teacher and I was being 'hauled over the coals' by a woman who showed neither interest in nor concern for either the teachers or the pupils in her charge. I suspect she felt that informing the education authority of any problems would be a reflection on her ability, or rather lack of it, as a headteacher. Even when she was brutally attacked by a parent, as described earlier, she refused to report the incident.

The Educational Psychologist arrived in the school at the beginning of an afternoon session. On entering my classroom Charlie was behaving in a most unruly manner, jumping on the chairs and the tables, screeching like a wild animal and flapping his arms up and down as if mimicking a bird: he was putting on a splendid performance. The visitor stood on the threshold in utter shock and, at that moment, Charlie darted out through the open doorway and sped down the corridor. The Psychologist, totally shaken, told me to go after the boy and he would look after the class.

At the afternoon break Charlie was escorted to his usual place of safety in the quadrangle, where he could not escape as he would if he were in the playground with the gates open. Here he could be observed from the school office. It was the only way I could get a break from him.

Having observed Charlie in the classroom and spent some time with him on his own the psychologist discussed the situation with me at the end of the afternoon. Well, to be truthful, it wasn't really a discussion. The man appeared traumatised by what he had seen. His comment:

"There is no way that I could cope with that child for ten minutes on his own. How on earth have you managed to cope with him in the class for a whole year and teach the other children?" It was not posed as a question for which he expected an answer!

Charlie was removed from the school within three weeks.

Unfortunately, it was just two weeks before the end of the school year so I hardly benefitted, but it did save the next teacher a similar experience. No more was said to me about the incident: the Headmistress never spoke of it again.

As must be apparent, Charlie, to a great extent, overshadowed this second year of my career as a primary school teacher. I do still wonder how I survived, for it was a constant struggle. However, survive I did and I suppose, as with all experiences, it made me stronger and more equal to the challenges of the future.

....

In the midst of all the turmoil there were some happy events during that school year. One such occasion was the Christmas Party.

December is an exciting time in any primary school and particularly with an infant class. The classrooms are at their most cheerful. The children themselves are very involved, making decorations, Christmas cards, calendars and paper hats. They take part in nativity plays and concerts and sing Christmas carols. This school was no different.

That Christmas there were colourful displays of children's work around the room, including their calendars, which would eventually be taken home. Using coloured sticky paper they made paper chains to string across the room. They cut out snowflake shapes for the windows and made paper party crowns from coloured tissue paper. The craft box was continually filled with empty cartons and packets, egg boxes and the tubes from the inside of toilet rolls (now banned from schools on the grounds of health and safety). The tubes were used as the centres for Christmas crackers. There were practices in the school hall to rehearse the party games and songs. A concert with songs and a nativity play was held for the parents.

Party day was always very special for the pupils. Of those who went home for lunch the boys would return 'scrubbed up' and looking their best, the girls would return in their party frocks. Of those who remained in school for lunch most had arrived in the morning either wearing their party gear or carrying things to change into. In the morning they also arrived armed with their contribution of food for the party. They would bring sandwiches, cakes and jelly. Nothing was specified: it was their choice. Amazingly this seemed to work well with a fair balance of each. Ice-cream was supplied by the school. It would come in large metal containers and would be brought round to the individual classrooms during the tea party. For drinks, the issue of free milk was reserved for the party tea that day.

As a special concession the teachers were allowed to 'bring a friend' to help on this occasion. Usually this friend would remain in the classroom to set out the party tea whilst the teachers escorted their pupils to the hall for party games and a sing-song. The parties were held for a whole year group at a time so there could be up to a hundred pupils at each party. The typical party games included 'In and Out the Shady Bluebells'; 'Oranges and Lemons'; 'Simon Says'; 'Pass the Parcel' and many more. To conclude the session in the hall there would be a singsong when the Headmistress would join us. This was one of the few occasions, apart from assemblies, when she actively participated. She had her own 'party piece' with the children. It was, 'One Finger, One Thumb Keep Moving' and, with all the actions, great fun for the children to join in.

On returning to our classrooms the tea party would begin

and I don't ever remember any children 'picking and poking' at the food, it was all devoured in a very short space of time. We all had a good time and, for once, there was someone to help tidy up.

Nowadays, schools still hold parties and concerts, but over the years some things have changed, mainly as a result of health and safety initiatives and strict copyright rules.

Children bringing food from home for parties is now generally discouraged. Instead the food is bought and brought in by the staff; not nearly as economical or exciting and incurring a good deal more hassle. Free school milk for all children has long gone and, in the case of milk for nursery pupils, it must be kept refrigerated and the temperature checked and recorded before it is served. How did we survive with school milk often sitting in the hot sun for hours before being consumed?

Certain items are now banned for use in craftwork. The tubes from the inside of toilet rolls, for instance, are now considered unhygienic.

The use of music and songs is strictly monitored to protect copyright laws, thereby making school productions much more expensive.

Parents and friends cannot simply be called in to help out on special occasions, as police checks must be in place first.

School halls can no longer be packed with parents coming along to see their offspring perform. Numbers are strictly controlled and ticketing often the only option: This latter, I do see as a very necessary regulation in terms of fire safety. Some of the other rulings have perhaps gone a little too far in the name of health and safety.

To End The Year:
A Shameful Act of Discrimination!

At the start of the school year several new staff were appointed including two male teachers who were newly qualified. One of them was very enthusiastic and competent, the other a rather lazy individual, entering the profession as a mature student and looking for an 'easy option'. Both successfully completed this, their probationary year. (Well, they had survived!)

The promotion system in schools in England at that time was as follows: Newly qualified teachers were on Scale 1 and many stayed at that level. Progression to Scale 2 was generally left to the discretion of the headteacher. To proceed further, up to Scale 3, an interview with the council was required: these Posts were advertised nationwide. Thereafter teachers could progress to Assistant or Deputy Head, then Headteacher, dependent on a successful application and interview. The basic salary scale extended over a period of 16 years. Additional remuneration for a promoted post was added to the basic scale so that it still took 16 years to reach the top salary no matter what position was held.

To return to our two gentlemen: the Headmistress, in her wisdom, offered each of them a Scale 2 post immediately on completion their probationary year. They both accepted.

The only criteria for this - they were men!

CHAPTER 9
Another School Year

The Saga Continues

In my third year I was once again faced with a new intake. This time they were not the very youngest children and some had even had some nursery experience. The Nursery Class in the school was now into its second year but the new nursery pupils were not to be admitted until the following week, thus giving the Nursery Teacher and her three assistants time to prepare. In consequence, these Nursery Nurses were available to assist the new class intakes on that first morning, which was a great help. They escorted the new pupils, one at a time, to their classrooms thus giving the Class Teachers a few moments to talk to and settle each child.

My class had almost reached its full complement of pupils and all was going well when a child was ushered through the door kicking and screaming. My heart sank. After a few minutes, when my shins were sore and already showing signs of bruising as a result of this child's tantrum, I thought,

"I really do not have to contend with this." I marched the offending child off to the Nursery so that he could be dealt with in isolation, away from the other children. He was returned later in the morning completely calm and presented little trouble from that moment on.

Although not all perfect 'little angels' this class was 'a dream' compared with the class of difficult and disturbed individuals I had encountered in my first two years. They settled quickly, adapting to their new routine without any major incidents.

Another Farce!

At some point during this year the school was designated an Educational Priority Area. This was based on the percentage of children attending the school who were from low-income families and thereby entitled to free school meals. One benefit of this: the teachers in the school were awarded an extra supplement on salaries, recognition of the additional burden associated with teaching in this area. It also meant that the school was allocated additional points for promoted posts. As a result, a Scale 3 position was on offer and was subsequently advertised. Several female members of staff were still reeling from the automatic promotion of the two male teachers to Scale 2 Posts. In retaliation, two of us, both only on a Scale 1, went ahead and applied for the Scale 3 Post. The Headmistress was furious but there was little she could do about it. (I don't think I was ever her 'flavour of the month' so I had nothing to lose).

Having applied for the job we were both offered an interview along with a teacher from another primary school. So, on a memorable day, three of us: the Headmistress and two teaching staff headed into the city to the Education Office. We were out of school for the entire morning. The result, no one was given a Scale 3 Post, but the two of us from the school were offered a Scale 2 each. What a farce! The Headmistress could have done this herself without resorting to interviews.

I realise I have painted a rather negative picture of our Headmistress but she did have a few redeeming features. One weekend I suffered with excruciating toothache and, as a result, had an emergency dental appointment first thing on the Monday morning. I had a tooth extracted under general anaesthetic but immediately afterwards went straight to school. I reported to her office to let her know I had arrived in the school, before going to my class. When she realised I'd had a general anaesthetic she insisted I sit down and rushed off to make me a cup of tea!

Staff meetings were a rare occurrence; in fact I can only ever remember attending one during my first three years in the school. We discussed various curricular issues, one being the teaching of arithmetic. It transpired that half the members of staff were applying a method known as 'decomposition'[3] for teaching subtraction and the other half, including myself, had no idea what it was. We were teaching according to the method of 'equal addition' that we, ourselves, had been taught in school and had never known anything different. It had never cropped up when I was at college or in any of the schools when I was on teaching practice. Oops!

Off to see the Queen

The Queen and the Duke of Edinburgh were passing through the city and it was expected that schoolchildren throughout would line the streets, waving flags and cheering. Excitement reigned in anticipation of this event but, since it was the first occasion that I had been involved in taking children out of school, I had reservations. There was, in fact, no need to worry. Of all the children I have ever taken out of school I can honestly say that the children from this school were the best behaved. I think that they were too mesmerized at the novelty of an 'outing' to think about

---

[3] 'Decomposition' and 'Equal Addition' are two different approaches to the teaching of addition. In the UK the former has become the preferred method as it is considered easier to demonstrate and explain to young children.

being naughty.

Each child, holding the hand of a partner, the whole school proceeded class by class for the half a mile or so to a point by the side of the road where the motorcade would pass by. They waited patiently for this significant event which, when it happened, lasted only a few seconds. But they were happy. They had seen the Queen and, from her open topped vehicle, she had waved to them and they had waved back.

Towards the end of my third year in the school the Headmistress announced that she would be leaving at the end of term. She had been appointed as Headteacher of another primary school in a much more prestigious part of the city, a world away from the challenges of the inner city.

We all waited in anxious anticipation for the appointment of a new Headteacher to lead us forward.

CHAPTER 10
A New Headteacher, a New Regime

Our new Headteacher could not have been more different from the previous Headmistress. Very experienced and ready for a challenge, she was enthusiastic and intent on being actively involved from the start.

Before the term began she was working hard within the school making a positive attempt to improve the environment, introducing colourful displays and objects of interest around the corridors. I must confess that we teachers were more than a little cynical at first, assuming that the children would soon demolish her painstaking efforts. However, this was not the case. Her efforts paid off, the children *were* interested; they talked about the items on display and were encouraged to make their own contributions.

Early in her first term the new Head called a meeting for those of us who held a Scale Two Post. She suggested that we should each have a particular responsibility within the school. This would ultimately enhance our C.V.'s should we wish to apply for further promotion in the future so, apart from supporting the current running of the school, it provided a boost for morale: a rather clever move.

I volunteered to take charge of reorganising the library: before entering the teaching profession I had worked for two years as a library assistant. I was very willing to be involved in this way, although it required time and effort, especially initially. With the help of my young son and a friend or two on a couple of Saturday mornings the books were sorted and coded and a system of borrowing set in place. Regrettably, the children were never allowed to take books home, even their reading books, but time was always made available for reading within the school day. Later, listening tapes were introduced and became part of the regular stock in the library.

Although not particularly musical myself, I have always enjoyed music and thought it important to identify and encourage musical talent in children. For this reason I set up a recorder group for some of the older pupils, the seven to nine year-olds. We managed to fit in practices during the lunchtime break. The group occasionally played at a school assembly, and at one point participated in an event at a concert hall in the city, along with recorder groups from other schools.

An Amusing Incident

Nature has always provided a point of interest in infant and junior classes. The displays set up by the Headteacher helped encourage the children to take notice of the things around them, sometimes adding their own contributions. However, a 'concrete jungle', as I have already described the environment around the school, does not really provide the ideal resource in this respect. We did our best.

During the autumn term, before all of the leaves had fallen I took my class out to observe the trees around the edge of the playground: a rare example of greenery within the estate. We looked up and talked about the different trees, collected fallen leaves, some of which were later pressed for display, and we looked at the tall trunks and examined the bark. In order to appreciate the different patterns of bark I demonstrated how to make a bark rubbing. Having returned to the classroom, I sent the children out into the playground in small groups, armed with the materials to make their own bark rubbings. Imagine my chagrin when I peered out of the door into the playground to find two of the children totally absorbed, busily taking a 'bark' rubbing of a telegraph pole.

Over the years schools, both primary and secondary, have been plagued with fads, fashions and government initiatives. In the 1970s rote learning of the multiplication tables became taboo. I never agreed with totally dismissing this method of teaching for, although I would not want children to spend vast amounts of time rote learning, I do believe that learning the tables and the odd poem in this way is quite reasonable, necessary even. Young children love repetition and can gain a real sense of achievement from learning in this way.

Our new Headteacher, being enthusiastic and having to answer to the Education Authority and HMI, was anxious to take on board the latest ideas. I doubt that the lady in question will be reading this but, if you are, I make no apology, although I do understand your stance. I confess, many a time I would open my classroom door, peer down the corridor to make sure no one was listening, before leading the class in the chanting of whichever of the tables we were focusing on that week.

When appointed to an independent school later in my career, it came to my attention that the learning of the multiplication tables by rote had never been abandoned in the private sector.

I wonder why!

At some point during the year we were informed that the school was to be painted and we were asked to choose the colours for our own classrooms. A good idea in theory, it gave us ownership, and having freshly decorated classrooms according to personal taste was really uplifting. I chose pale yellow. The problem arose in later years when teachers moved rooms and were faced with someone else's colour scheme. This was especially disconcerting for the person who took over the room previously occupied by one of the male members of staff who had chosen to have his room painted in shades of psychedelic pink.

On the subject of redecorating the school, can anyone tell me why it is that workmen invariably arrive at the beginning of a school term? For several weeks each class in turn was 'decanted' to the library whilst the painters moved from one classroom to another: a massive upheaval for the whole school. The children probably thought this was a great idea, but not so the teachers.

Things definitely improved with the new Headteacher. Having someone at the helm showing an interest in the pupils and the staff had an enormous impact on the smooth running of the school. Having a salary increase in recognition of the difficulties in teaching in a school in a deprived area provided added incentive: The problems we faced were positively acknowledged and rewarded. It made a difference.

Promotion!

For the first few years of my career I taught classes of the youngest pupils. The very first class, as stated, I took through to the following year. Thereafter I continued with reception classes or early stages, until eventually I decided I would like a change and requested a class of older children (juniors). I clearly remember parents, on hearing that I was to teach a class of eight year olds, congratulating me on my promotion. This I must emphasise loud and clear was not the case. The responsibility for teaching the very youngest children should never be underestimated.

Juniors
(The Mid-Primary School Stages)

Teaching slightly older children in this inner city school had certain compensations. It was policy at this time to assess children at the age of seven, and such was the nature of the catchment area that many pupils, as outlined earlier, were ultimately considered too poor to continue in mainstream education so were transferred to an E.S.N. School. I have to say that being relieved of these children was beneficial, bearing in mind that there was no additional 'support for learning' within the school.

However, that is not to say that all the problems were removed. The remaining pupils were still mostly from deprived family backgrounds. Many were neglected, some were abused and a few were under care orders from the local authority.

Ruby

Ruby was a delightful child. An intelligent girl, she worked hard and never presented any problems in the classroom. Her family background, however, was desperate: She frequently spent periods in a care home or with foster parents.

On the very last day of the autumn term, immediately before we broke up for the Christmas holidays, she came to chat with me before leaving. She intimated that she feared neither of her parents would be at home when she returned that afternoon and that she would probably be taken into care for the holiday period. I was both shocked and saddened at the thought of this lovely girl spending, what should be a wonderful family time, away from her own home and family. Sure enough, when Ruby returned to school after that Christmas break, I learned that her prediction had indeed been correct. She had gone home that last day of the term to be taken away by virtual strangers and placed in the care of a foster family for the entire duration of the holiday.

Life surely does not get a great deal tougher than that for a young child.

Off to the Seaside

On the retirement of our Deputy Headmistress, a new Deputy Head was appointed. A man. He had sandy/red hair and a very fair complexion to match. This manifested itself in an unfortunate characteristic: the slightest problem and he would blush, turning a very deep shade of pink. He was a very pleasant natured gentleman, and this being his first promoted post he was anxious to make a good impression.

On perhaps the hottest day of the summer term, soon after taking up his appointment, our new Deputy Head was placed in charge of a trip to the seaside. As we gathered in the hall early in the morning in question the Headteacher sent out a clear message. There was to be no going in the sea.

The majority of children had never seen the sea. For many it was possibly the first time they had ever ventured off the estate. Exactly what did she imagine they were going to do? Anyway, off we set, over a hundred children with their class teachers, all in the trusted charge of the newly appointed Deputy Head. The temperature was rising, soon exceeding 90 degrees.

Halfway through the journey - sudden PANIC. The first coach halted and the second followed suit. The Deputy Head announced he had forgotten to load the school milk into the coach. This was the sole source of liquid refreshment to be consumed by the pupils along with their packed lunches, which, I hasten to add, *were* on board.

What a catastrophe.

The poor man was consumed by guilt and his face had turned to something resembling the colour of a beetroot. He would have to telephone the school. Not too easy a task with no mobile 'phones and few public telephones en route. We suggested he buy some orange juice, but he insisted he needed permission from the Headteacher. Next stop, a telephone kiosk. Permission sought and granted. Next stop, a shop.

Calm prevailed once more and we continued on our journey to the seaside, where awaited the next drama.

It was uncomfortably hot and we were all grateful to be off the coach at last. We gathered our classes, visited the toilets, and re-assembled before making our way down to the beach. For a few minutes order was maintained. However, it did not last. There was a long gently sloping path leading down to the shore and, as the children reached the top of the slope in sight of the sea their excitement reached its height, they could not be restrained. They were off! Nothing was going to stop them. I raced ahead in an effort to prevent the inevitable. The sea had beckoned. I managed to shout to them, "take off your shoes and socks". To try to stop them going into the sea was not an option - it was too late. Quickly I whipped off my skirt and t-shirt to reveal a bright yellow bikini. I, at least, had come prepared. How thankful I was, for it meant that I could wade into the sea and position myself behind the children. One or two of my colleagues were similarly prepared and joined me to form a protective barrier. The rest remained by the water's edge. The children were safe and for the next half hour or so they were happy to splash and paddle and enjoy this unfamiliar experience. Yes, some did get fairly well soaked but most were content to get their feet wet or simply dip their toes into the water. Once the Deputy Head had recovered from his initial shock and returned to his normal colour he relaxed for a while. His next trauma was a fear that the children would all suffer with sunstroke and he would lose his job.

Eventually, we herded all of the children safely onto the beach where they soon dried off and played happily in the sand before heading back up the long slope for a packed lunch and orange juice.

On the way back to school in the coach we had a traditional old-fashioned singsong. We had all had a good time. Well, almost all!

Safely back in school the children carried memories of their trip to the seaside for a very long time. Their written news the following day was inevitably illustrated with their teacher wearing a bright yellow bikini. When the Headteacher came to see the work they had produced of their day out I received a rather sceptical glance but nothing was said.

More Outings

Outings for these children were not a regular occurrence and despite her instructions not to allow the children into the sea on the memorable seaside trip, our Headteacher *was* the instigator of the trips we had. She was anxious to encourage experiences to broaden the pupils' education and very supportive of any extra curricular initiatives. Opportunities for the children were still limited under our new Head but at least they existed.

Another day out that I remember was a trip to the zoo. We were on a double decker bus and I was on the top deck with my class, so we had a splendid panoramic view of the surrounding area. We had not travelled very far from the estate and out into the countryside when we passed a field of cows. The children were bursting with excitement at this unfamiliar sight and one child shouted out, "hey, miss, miss, are we at the zoo?"

As intimated earlier, these children were exceedingly well behaved when out of school. Of course they were excited: there were moments when they could hardly contain themselves. But generally they were simply 'in awe' of being out of school and in their own way very appreciative of the experience.

In 1962 the Sunshine Coach Programme was launched. It was an initiative of the Variety Club of Great Britain, a charity which helps sick and disadvantaged children. Over the years thousands of coaches have been donated to schools all over the UK, schools in deprived areas as well as special needs schools. Being a designated Education Priority Area we were granted a Sunshine Coach. As I recall, we contributed a little ourselves through some fundraising activities such as jumble sales, raffles and a sponsored silence (what a brilliant idea). Some of the teachers in the school volunteered their services as drivers and were trained for this purpose. We tried to give as many children as possible the opportunity of a trip out using this newly acquired facility but since the coach could only carry around 16 pupils at a time, this required careful arrangement for staffing.

On one occasion I was able to take some of the pupils in my

class for a half-day trip out into the countryside. On the return journey we stopped off at my house for orange juice and biscuits. The children were delighted and again on their best behaviour. It wasn't until afterwards I realised that some of the glasses I had used to serve the juice were, in fact, my grandmother's best crystal.

An Inspector Calls

A Survey of Children's Learning

During my sixth year in the school a countrywide survey took place in order to assess pupils' learning. A random selection of schools was chosen from across the country. Our school was one of two selected from our area and from within the school two classes were identified according to the surnames of the teachers, beginning at a random place in the alphabet. My class, along with the class of one of the male teachers, was selected in this way.

We had plenty of notice, from the beginning of the autumn term to the middle of the spring term: too long as far as I was concerned. It is stressful enough for staff when there is a general inspection of the whole school but, in this case, only two classes were to be scrutinised. The burden was immense but not shared. This inspection was to be carried out by two HMI's over the course of a week. The other classes would be left alone to carry on as normal. We were assured that the inspectors were only concerned with the pupils' learning and not with the teachers' performance. Well really! Just how were they going to assess the learning of the pupils' without considering the direction from the teacher? If that was the case why didn't they give us the week off.

Our very enthusiastic Headteacher was anxious that her school would be seen to be providing the best possible education for the children. She was supportive throughout the year giving encouragement whilst ensuring that all was well.

After months of anxious anticipation the dreaded week was upon us. The two gentlemen were very pleasant and went out of their way to make us feel comfortable about their visit. They explained the aims and implications of the survey and set a schedule for their classroom observations. Only one inspector would be present in a classroom at any one time.

During the course of three days they each observed a number of sessions in my class and did, in fact, make a cursory visit to the other classes in the school. I had two 'half-hearted' criticisms, one from each of the two inspectors. One, on observing a session where the children were working in groups, suggested that it might have been preferable for them to be working as a class. The other, on observing a class lesson, thought that the pupils should have been working in groups. Well, I suppose they had to find something to say.

I was given the opportunity to discuss various aspects of the learning with each of the inspectors and to chat with them generally. Neither of them were primary school trained nor did they have any experience of teaching young children. Both had taught in secondary schools.

At the end of three days they discussed their findings with the Headteacher before going away to write their official reports. The Headteacher was delighted to inform me that they were well satisfied with the work that was going on in my class. They had noted from examples of the children's work throughout the year that what they saw was a continuum of general good practice.

A Demonstration Lesson

It is not often that an Inspector or Advisor is sufficiently brave to do a demonstration lesson. Normally they come into school, observe, criticize and write a report, which can often make teacher's feel less than adequate. They rarely venture to show us how it should be done. The only instance that I remember this happening was an Advisor for Physical Education who visited this inner city school for the sole purpose of doing exactly that. He did not come into the school to observe any of the staff. He came purely to share his own expertise.

My junior class at the time were as excited as I was at the prospect. I was interested to learn from his ideas and it was a novelty for the children to have a lesson with an expert in this field. Under my supervision the children changed into their PE kit in the classroom ready for this lesson. Obviously it was not part of the Advisor's remit to oversee this precursor to the lesson and this is where the admirable gentleman had a significant advantage. Had he been in the same situation as that of class teacher his task would have increased somewhat in difficulty. To explain:

Whilst most of the children were getting ready one boy was having a tantrum. He hid under a desk refusing to get changed. As he remained cowering in this position I escorted the rest of the class to the gym and quickly relayed to the advisor that I was having problems with one of the boys and would have to return to my classroom to attend to him. When I attempted to lure the boy from under the desk he ran out of the room screaming, fled into the playground and away. I followed in pursuit of the young miscreant, eventually catching up with him several streets away. Finally, exhausted, he calmed down and I led him back to the school, by which time I had missed a good part of the advisor's lesson. What I did see of it was impressive: I was just sorry that I had missed so much.

I wonder how the man would have fared had he been expected to deal with the whole scenario as well as take the lesson.

More Tales from the Juniors

Dealing with children who have specific problems can be a real challenge in the classroom and especially with a large class in cramped conditions. During one school year, with classes of around 35, each teacher had to accept extra pupils from another class whose teacher was off sick. This brought the number of children in my class up to 40. To exacerbate the situation further these extra children were particularly poor academically. They had been deliberately assigned to one small class as a means of allowing a better teacher:pupil ratio. This was done in the hope that it would give them the additional support to help them achieve. So, it was rather ironic that they all spent a whole term in even bigger classes whose sizes were now inflated by their presence. In the midst of this 'crisis' I had a child in my own class who was showing signs of what appeared to be epilepsy, although as yet it had not been diagnosed. The girl in question was quiet and reserved. She was from a non-problematic, very caring family background and had no learning or behavioural difficulties.

At first the fits were hardly noticeable, resembling petit mal seizures, lasting just a few seconds, but over the course of the term they became much more serious. She would stare into space, sway back and forth and lose consciousness. If I recognised the onset of a 'fit' I would guide her out into the corridor away from the other children but, more often than not it was too late, I had to stand by and hope that I could protect her from injury. In the event of a serious incident an older sibling would accompany her home where she would 'sleep it off'. The 'fits' became more frequent, often occurring several times a week, and they began to take a stranger form. She would climb up onto a chair or a desk. I would stand as close as I could to catch or guide her as she regained consciousness.

One day, just as the bell rang for the end of the morning session, I observed her acting strangely. (Most of the children were already out of the door so I hastened the rest of them on their way.) She swayed against a cupboard, knocking over a tin of black powder paint and proceeded to climb up onto a chair, then a desk. Suddenly she fell and missed striking her head against the corner of a cupboard by a fraction of an inch.

Trembling from the shock, I led the dazed child to the school office. Her mother was called to take her home for the remainder of the day. Something had to be done.

Fortunately the situation had been monitored over the previous weeks and, armed with records from myself together with her own observations, the mother was able to persuade her family doctor to have her assessed. Medication was subsequently prescribed to control the illness, an outcome that initially the family had hoped to avoid.

Ellen

The nursery, which opened in my second year at the school

had been financed by the local authority specifically to help address the poverty and vulnerability of families within the school's catchment area. Priority places were allocated to children who were considered to be 'at risk' as identified by social workers and health visitors.

One such referral to that first nursery class was a girl called Ellen. She was a delightful and exceptionally bright child whom I had the pleasure of teaching in the reception class straight after her year in the nursery and again for the autumn term just before I resigned from my post at the school.

It is easy to imagine that children from so-called 'deprived' backgrounds are academically poorer than their 'better off' counterparts. This is not true. Certainly, they often lack opportunities, and may not have the plethora of books and educational experiences within the home that the so-called privileged have. Nevertheless, children can absorb a good deal within the school day. Also, in the 1970s children had the advantage of more exercise: they went out to play. Being in school all day should surely be enough for any young child without having the stress of homework, or being bombarded with 'education' at home. Compared with the so called 'well-off' children of today, who seem permanently attached to TV's, computers, mobile 'phones and tablets, many were not so badly off. Ellen was definitely a case in point. In addition, she was clearly 'loved' despite what I am about to relate.

During the 1970s a Home Start initiative began. Teachers were encouraged to visit some of the most vulnerable children in their own homes in order to build links between the home and the school. It was thought that this would help create a positive attitude in parents towards their child's education and teaching staff. Under this initiative I visited several pupils in their homes.

Ellen had been admitted to the nursery as a welfare case. A social worker had visited the home and discovered a dead dog in the bed: hence the referral. The family was very poor and with Ellen and two other young children under school age the mother was not coping too well. Ellen's was one of the homes I visited.

Ellen's family lived fairly close to the school. Their home was the upper floor of a two-storey end terrace house accessed via their own front door and staircase. The walls of the stairway were damp and covered in mould. On reaching the top of the stairs I remained on the threshold of a dismal over-crowded living area. The stench was sickening; the dimness and clutter claustrophobic; there was no space to sit down. I had never before entered a house that was so depressing. The mother, poorly clad and aged beyond her years, presented a similar image to that of the room, but she was very pleasant and exhibited a caring, loving attitude towards her offspring.

To say that I was shocked would be an understatement. There, amidst the filth, the squalor and the stench was a respect for me and for the school and a genuine understanding and regard for the children. It brought to light a vivid realisation that outward appearance is not necessarily a reflection of inward attitude and warmth: A real eye-opener.

As well as Ellen's family home I visited a few others, but hers was probably the worst in terms of the lack of cleanliness. Yet Ellen's ability, her behaviour and her confidence, despite her background, were exemplary.

On visiting other homes, what struck me was the frequent presence of a colour television set in the corner of the room. Given such abject poverty, in families considered so needy as to warrant free school meals for their offspring, I was amazed that such a luxury was possible. At the time, a colour television was not an item I owned, nor was it considered a priority amongst my colleagues. We were struggling to buy our own homes and the latest TV model was not at the top of our list of essentials. The term 'must have' had not yet reared its ugly head. I was baffled and saddened by what I considered to be an outrageous miss-use of money, where it seemed acceptable for children to go without proper food and clothing whilst parents thought nothing of spending on such extravagances. The situation has not improved over the years. Families are now slaves to the latest technology, forever upgrading to the most recent gadget.

Ellen was a pupil of mine in her first official school year having spent the previous year in the newly opened nursery. I taught her again a few years later by which time she was eight or nine. She had continued to flourish throughout the intervening years and was fortunate to be in a class with several other bright girls. It was also a class in which there were a number of children who had been identified as vulnerable. Ellen came into this category. Although living at home they were under the watchful eye of the local authority. In some instances I was asked to look out for bruising, more likely to be observed as children changed for PE. Anything untoward had to be noted and reported.

Some of these children presented no problem whatsoever, others were a constant worry. One child cuddled up to me every morning and needed consoling and re-assuring before any teaching could begin. Sometimes she would disappear for several days at a time. In the case of this child a referral was made to the Children's Panel, not an uncommon occurrence in this school. Shortly afterwards she disappeared again and a search for her whereabouts ensued. She was eventually traced. Her mother had taken her to another city over 100 miles away and she had, thankfully, been enrolled in another school.

This was to be my final term in this school. As a result of my husband accepting a new job we were moving to another part of the UK. The class, though a challenge as indicated, was nevertheless a delight and I was given a heart-rending send off. Practically every child presented me with a gift on the last week of the term. Ellen handed me some money, a few coins, which I was most reluctant to accept. However, when she explained that she wanted me to buy stamps so that I could write to her, it was impossible to refuse.

So ended my first teaching post: six and a half very challenging years with some joy and much heartache.

As a result of the problems the staff were very close and very supportive. I have some happy memories. Many of the pupils did achieve, despite their 'deprived' background, and that was satisfying. But, I was tired, I was ready for a break, for some time to relax and reflect. The pressure of upwards of 35 children in a class with so many social and emotional needs, where the job becomes more like that of a social worker than a teacher, is demanding and draining. Specialist support was nonexistent and for the first three years, under a Headmistress whose answer to the problems was 'ignore them and they will go away', the strain on staff was tremendous.

Postscript:
Ellen did write to me and for a year or so we corresponded regularly.

15.2.79.

Dear Mrs ....

I am so sorry that i haveint been able to write to you because i have had no paper and lots of homework But now i have found some paper and i am able to write to you I hope you had a nice christmas and new year especely in the bad weather. I hope you are having good weather because we are having awfull weather. Did you get nice presents? Because we did. An And on May 30th i am going to the lakedistricts with the brownies We will be going from 7.30 am untill 9.00 pm, we will be going on a steam train, a boat and other places but i will write to you before then.

Lots of love and best wishes from ....

P.T.O.

A Letter From Ellen

The Influence of the Headteacher:

Analysing my experience up to this point, both as a student and as a young teacher in my first teaching post, it is apparent that the Headteacher in every case was crucial to the smooth running of the school.

The school I attended for my first teaching practice was warm and friendly. The children were from a mix of working class backgrounds, not desperately poor but certainly not affluent. The Headmistress cared deeply for the pupils, making it a priority to know them individually. She took her turn on playground duty, opened her room to them as a library, talked to them about their work and made them feel special on their birthdays. This helped motivate both teachers and pupils and encouraged mutual respect. The daily assemblies generated a closeness that would be difficult to match in a larger establishment.

By contrast, the school I was allocated for my final teaching practice was 'cold'. The staff were wary, constantly 'on edge'; the pupils nervous and afraid; the parents alienated. There are situations in life where to 'rule with a rod of iron' may be appropriate but it was totally unnecessary and counter productive in this small infant school. If there were assemblies I don't remember any of them. The Headmistress, a spinster, had no life outside the school, so in school she behaved as a dictator ruling her domain. She needed to possess us all, we belonged to her: An incredibly unhealthy stance.

Children, especially young children, rely on their class teachers. As the one adult with whom they spend a high proportion of their time their class teacher becomes a 'significant' person in their lives. If that person is unsure of themselves this will be relayed to the children in their charge. None of this is beneficial to their education.

For the first three years in my first teaching post the Headmistress was distant. She did not bother the staff much but neither did she support them. I'm sure she felt that if she stayed cocooned in her room all the time then all the problems would go away. But, in any school, and particularly one in a 'deprived' area with numerous desperate families, the problems don't go away. A Headteacher is the one person who needs to be in control, who can discuss with class teachers and liaise with the authorities as necessary.

Every child is deserving of a decent education. But, in order for this to happen, pupils with severe learning difficulties as well as those who are disruptive as a result of serious social and emotional problems need to be assessed and either removed from the classroom situation or else properly supported within it. In assuming a strategy of avoidance our Headmistress was letting down every child in the school, denying them the environment for learning which should have been theirs by right.

The following three years presented a distinct contrast. The new Headteacher made herself available for both staff and pupils. She made difficult pupils her concern, thus sharing the burden and helping as appropriate. She aroused in us an enthusiasm that had previously been lacking, introducing new innovations and sharing her expertise. As a result we were able to improve on the quality of education provided. We were never going to be able to perform miracles but the difference in standards was remarkable.

PART 3

NEW HORIZONS

CHAPTER 11
The Country Schools

20 December 1977. My first teaching post finally came to an end. We were moving away to join my husband who had been offered a job in another part of the UK.

I was exhausted but free and looked forward to a new venture. Later on that evening friends waved me and my son off on the overnight train to Scotland where we arrived the following morning in the pitch dark. It was the shortest day of the year. A few days earlier the furniture plus my car, a little Fiat 500, had disappeared in the removal van on its journey north.

After several tough years in an inner city school it was a joy to relax and take some time out. However, I had decided to study with the Open University and embarked on courses leading to certificates in Language Development and Reading Development. In order to fulfill the requirements of these courses I needed access to a school so, having registered with GTC (General Teaching Council for Scotland), I requested and was granted permission to spend some time in the local country school. The Headteacher was delighted. It gave him an afternoon away from the classroom to get on with administrative duties. During the summer term I did some relief teaching and after the summer holidays I began work as 'Head Teacher's Relief', spending one day a week in each of three country schools.

Each of the schools had just two teachers, covering the entire primary school stages with children aged four to 12. Generally the Headteacher would take the upper stages, usually Primary Five to Primary Seven, although depending on numbers, sometimes Primary Four as well. Each school had a total of around 30 children. So, from classes of around 35 pupils all at one stage, I now had classes of 12 to 16 covering at least three stages.

When I arrived at the first school for my first day I was in total awe. What a contrast! An entire school with fewer pupils than I'd had in one class. A classroom looking out over fields and hills: an incredible sense of freedom. In the second school the view of the surrounding countryside from the classroom was even more spectacular. The third school was again situated way out in the countryside although the windows were too high to provide a view.

In each of the three schools peripatetic teachers came to take lessons in Art, Drama, Music, P.E. and Home Economics: in some cases just for one term in the year, in others for the whole year. There was also Learning Support.

The 'catchment' area for each of the schools was, of course, rural. Two of them were close to very small villages but most children arrived by mini bus or taxi from the surrounding area. Several lived on farms and a few were incomers, new to the area. Having such a wide age range in such small schools resulted in a real family atmosphere. This proved a bonus at playtimes: there was no playground supervision but the children cared for each other and there was never a problem. The older children were trusted to look after the younger ones and mishaps were brought to the notice of the staff immediately.

The Headteacher in my 'Tuesday' school had been in the police force and adopted a 'no nonsense' attitude with the children, but he was also a lot of fun and, because there were so few pupils, this was possible: they knew the limits. The curriculum was rather rigid. For example, every morning the whole class wrote in their diaries; all of the children in a year group were on the same reading book. A strict routine was followed. Aside from the basics and the specialist teaching some of the learning was based on 'projects'. At the beginning of each term a large box would arrive from the Education Department Library containing books and support materials for that term's selected project.

So, given that the mountain of curriculum guidelines in the form of 5-14 had not yet descended upon us and the era of computers had not yet dawned, things were really rather well organised. We were not yet overburdened with paperwork and bureaucracy and were able to focus on the real job of teaching. Two of the boys from this particular group of children were eventually to gain places at Oxford University so, for all that it was a little stilted and archaic, there was obviously not much wrong with the system.

At this school the mid-day meals were cooked 'in house' so the cook was very much a part of the staff. Pupils and teachers all sat down together for dinner in the kitchen / dining room.

One day there was a moment of panic when the vegetables for the dinner had not arrived. No problem. The Headteacher nipped out of school, across the road and over the fence into the 'park' (i.e. field). He gathered some neaps (swedes) and, hey presto, we had our veg! I was speechless. What would they have thought of this in the inner city school? Seeing my look of amazement I was assured that this was all in order. The Headteacher was a friend of the farmer and, in any case, neaps were widely used as 'animal feed'.

For many of the children in the country schools their 'first language' was the local dialect spoken at home. Yet, in the classroom they adapted immediately to Standard English. On one occasion I decided to analyse the local 'twang'. I sent two farmers' boys to a quiet room with a tape recorder to discuss their weekend activities. It really was amusing. They began in Standard English but, after a few minutes, lapsed into the local dialect: a completely different language.

On another occasion we were looking at examples of homophones (words that sound the same but are spelled differently and have a different meaning). Here's where my knowledge (or lack of it) of the local dialect let me down. Amongst other examples I wrote on the blackboard YOU and EWE. The children were puzzled and when I emphasised the words giving the same pronunciation they began to laugh. In many parts of Scotland the word EWE is pronounced as YOW (rhyming with HOW).

My 'Wednesday' school was similar as regards the curriculum but quite different in its leadership. The Headmistress lived in the schoolhouse, which was next to the school grounds. Frequently she would come into school in the morning, settle her class and go home to have a bath. Every morning we had extended breaks. She brought in cheese and biscuits or home baking. It was a real tea party. The children happily played outside, or indoors if it was wet, and nobody seemed to mind. Though not a strict disciplinarian the children again knew their limits, they appeared happy and the work was always done. What can one say?

The leadership in my 'Friday' school was rather more chaotic. Children were allowed to 'leave the room' without bothering to ask and were altogether too familiar with their teacher. They did, however, settle down, and it was here that I had the freedom to carry out much of my work in connection with the Open University courses on reading and language development.

One of the boys in the class was a dedicated ballet dancer and very much respected by his peers as he also played football. Being exceedingly supple and agile in his movements, he was the best goalkeeper.

The children were local, mostly from families who had been in the area for generations. One boy always appeared much more scruffy than the rest, rather 'unkempt'. He would be the child to whom I would be inclined to offer the spare bottle of milk. Imagine my astonishment when one day his mother came to collect him early from school because they were going to have afternoon tea with the Queen Mother. He was, apparently, the son of the local Laird.

To conclude, the two years I spent covering these country schools provided some of the most enjoyable experiences of my teaching career. The children were a joy: the numbers were such that it was possible to get to know them properly and to relax without sacrificing control. There was a superb support system in place with specialist teachers who, as well as enriching the education for the pupils, also relayed the latest 'gossip' to the staff. This helped balance the tendency to become insular and isolated. At this time education was as yet relatively uncluttered by government initiatives and bureaucracy.

Homework consisted of reading a page or two of the reading scheme book, learning a few spellings and perhaps a few 'sums', never more. I am horrified at the amount of homework expected of very young children nowadays, in some cases several hours a week. I would have thought the school day long enough without burdening them in this way. An hour or two kicking a football would be far more beneficial. The country children had the advantage of breathing the fresh country air and, up to this point in time, were allowed out to play without the constant eye of an adult watching their every move.

The Scottish education system was recognised as one of the best in the world but, sadly, this was not to last.

CHAPTER 12
Back to Full Time Teaching

The Primary Five Crew

After two years as a relief teacher I secured a permanent teaching post in a 'satellite' town. The catchment area for the school was predominately middle class. It was originally a small village but it had expanded beyond recognition with new housing, forming a huge estate of mostly privately owned homes, taking over the once rural area. As in the country schools there was still the advantage of specialist teachers and learning support. Expectations were high and pupils generally performed accordingly. Although it did not offer the same closeness as the rural schools it was nevertheless a happy place with a real sense of community.

In my first year I was allocated a Primary Five class. I very much enjoyed working with this middle primary school stage: I felt really comfortable with the children. It was a joy to have my own class again and good to be able to get down to the job of teaching without having to be a social worker. The planning of lessons was manageable and purposeful.

The Primary Five children were a delight. They were a class that really 'jelled', referring to themselves as 'The Primary Five Crew'. Apart from one boy, who sometimes acted a little strangely, there were no really difficult or problem children in the class. A sole incident stands out when the aforementioned child proved rather awkward:

The class had swimming for a term, which was quite an adventure. It meant a whole morning out of school every week, beginning with a bus journey of several miles. At the pool the children were organised into groups with non-swimmers at the shallow end under one instructor and the swimmers at the deep-end with another instructor. On this particular day the boy, a non-swimmer, decided to take a leap into the deep end of the pool. Although he was well aware of what he was doing, he somehow thought he would be all right. He wasn't! He had to be rescued by the attendant who dived into the pool and brought him to the side and thence to safety. In a state of utter shock the very frightened child rushed off to the changing rooms, locked himself in a cubicle, and refused to come out. When, after much persuasion, he still stayed put, I had to contact the school to let them know that we would be late back for dinner. Eventually, the pool attendant managed to talk him round, but it was quite a performance. He had not calculated the risk involved in his actions and had got a real scare. He didn't attempt it again.

In Primary Five the pupils had lessons in cookery as part of what was then referred to as 'Home Economics'. One morning they were making macaroni cheese and on returning to the classroom just before lunchtime they brought their 'offerings' for me to try. I was invited to taste three different samples and asked which I preferred. They were 'over the moon' when, unbeknown to me, I chose their genuine 'homemade' version. The other two were 'tinned'.

As part of the math's curriculum the class were doing some practical work on weighing and measuring, including producing a chart on their own weight and height. At this time, although we were teaching the metric system, most people still used imperial weights and measures and the pupils were thus much more familiar with this method. One girl in the class, who was rather taller than the other girls, made the following request:

"Can you measure me in feet and inches so that everyone will know how tall I am, but can you weigh me in kilograms so that no one will know how heavy I am?"

Well, that just about summed up the general attitude towards the metric system. Money was different as the changeover happened over night: there was no option. But, even today, many persist in referring to imperial weights and measures.

The main highlight of that year was the Christmas Concert. I had asked the girls about the playground games and songs I had heard them singing when they were outside at lunchtime. They gave a demonstration in the classroom and decided it might make a good act as part of the concert at Christmas. They made up an itinerary and put on a superb performance: quite an original idea. The boys, who were mostly football fanatics, had their own football related theme, as one might guess.

Primary Four

The following school year I had a Primary Four class. They were a delightful bunch until chaos descended in the form of Kevin.

Kevin

One morning the Headteacher came to my classroom with a 'new' boy. He had been attending a school in one of the roughest areas of the city. His appearance itself immediately set him apart from the other pupils: his behaviour was about to confirm the real difference. He shouted and swore, looked at his fellow classmates with distain and did not respond to discipline. Efforts by the other children to befriend him were not reciprocated. This was a clear illustration of the way in which one disruptive child can cause mayhem in an otherwise smooth running establishment. We are often told by 'the powers that be' that every child deserves a good mainstream education, that all children should be integrated. Well, that's true. But, it is not just the unruly child who deserves the best that education can offer, it is *every* child: it is all those who want to learn, who are prepared to work hard. One child who is out of control cannot easily be placated within a class of 30. There needs to be some system in place to deal with disruptive children outside the classroom, so that they may eventually be properly integrated without ruining the opportunities of others. In the case of this child the whole neighbourhood suffered. He was, at one point, found in the company of his older brother attempting to break into the local bank.

It was somewhat of a relief that the family did not stay for long in the area, but that does not solve the issue, it simply transfers the problem elsewhere.

To return to normality, one of the boys in this class had a physical disability. His little arms ended at the elbow with deformed hands on which numerous operations were being performed to give a better chance of effective manipulation. Despite the pain he must often have been suffering he joined in everything. His handwriting was better than most, he played football as heartily as any of the other lads and he always appeared happy. After a few days his deformity was simply not noticed. I met him several years later, a pleasant, handsome young man who made a point of approaching me. He was working in an office, was very involved in sports and by no means a victim of his disability.

CHAPTER 13

A Change of School

After two years in this school I transferred to a village school. The catchment area was similar although there were probably more children from the surrounding countryside. Once again a far cry from the inner city school, although not completely problem free.

It was around this time in my career that significant changes began to take place in primary education. Firstly, forward planning, in accordance with regional guidelines, became much more structured. That, in itself, was not bad thing, but when it reached the stage where we had to complete 37 sheets of A4 paper for forward planning at the beginning of each term in addition to the regular weekly planning, it was becoming burdensome. And that was merely a taste of what was to come in the shape of the impending 5-14 Programme (The National Curriculum in England, Wales and Northern Ireland).

Primary Three and Primary Four

For the next five years I remained at the Primary Three and Primary Four stages, which I enjoyed very much. A 'bright' child at Primary One or Two can present quite a challenge as they need to 'be stretched' but lack the maturity to be left to work without constant intervention. However, as they move up the school they are capable of getting on with tasks independently.

One such child in Primary Three, having completed the set work for a morning, was focused on a task that involved reading a short story on which to answer questions without referring back. Another boy in the class noticed how quickly he was reading. He came to me very excited and eager to point out the reader,

"Look Miss, Miss. See how fast he is reading". He continued to gape, wide eyed at the other boy.

The reader was indeed reading quickly and, on checking, he was totally in command of what he was reading. The second boy, from an original travelling family, was genuinely full of admiration for his classmate. He was one of the most polite, well-behaved pupils I ever taught.

At one point during this school year an opportunity arose to take some pupils to a ballet to see a performance of 'The Nutcracker'. It was not compulsory and was to take place after the end of a school day. To my surprise four of the boys, but none of the girls in the class wanted to go. So, along with some children from other classes, we set off in a hired coach. The boys were totally absorbed in the performance. Three of them were already learning to play a musical instrument. It is a joy to see children of this age group so enthusiastic about music.

The Chicken and the Egg

Approaching Easter time with this same Primary Three class, and being topical, I decided to bring some eggs into school to be incubated. At the time we were living out in the country and kept chickens, so I had experienced the wonder of seeing newly hatched chicks: the children would love it. With the help of the janitor we set up the incubator and the eggs were put in place, the timing such that they would hatch just at the start of the new school term after the Easter holidays.

On arrival at school towards the end of the holidays I was dismayed to discover that nothing was happening. The janitor had been keeping a watchful eye on things but something had gone wrong. Not to disappoint the children, on my way to school on the first day of the term, I made a detour to a local hatchery where I purchased some newly hatched chicks and subsequently deposited them in the incubator at school. The children were absolutely delighted: it was magical. However, I had not totally got away with my cunning scheme. One boy in the class was a farmer's son and I had certainly not succeeded in 'pulling the wool over his eyes'. A lovely lad, he was very discreet in disclosing his suspicions. As the rest of the class disappeared out to play he came and whispered to me, "those were not the eggs we put there before Easter". I put a finger to my lips to indicate, "that can be our secret". He grinned, gave a 'knowing' look, and went away quite happily.

A Visit from the Inspectorate

During a year when I had a Primary Four class the Inspectors visited the school. Although we had plenty of warning it was an intense time for the staff. Reports by HMI were made public and no one wanted to let either the school or themselves down.

That year I had a child in the class who presented a particular challenge. He had been adopted, along with his younger brother, by a couple who ran a local cafe. The two boys were quite a handful having had a very disturbing start to life. On the week that the Inspectors were in school the mother, rather cunningly I thought, kept her son off school, covering the absence with a convincing letter of explanation. Perhaps this is not the best approach to a visit from the Inspectorate, but I have to admit that I was grateful.

The visit went well: we were given an excellent report.

The Introduction of the Computer into the Primary School

The Prime Minister, Margaret Thatcher, had pledged that by 1984 there should be a computer in every primary school. Well, one computer in a school of well over 200 pupils did not really have much impact, and it was a while before we had a computer for each class. When we finally reached this stage it was a complete nightmare. The first computer available for the use of each class, was the Sinclair ZX Spectrum with a capacity of 16K. It was expected that every child should be able to perform certain tasks on this machine - a totally unrealistic expectation given the temperamental nature of this piece of technology and the complete absence of any training for teaching staff. Although it undoubtedly had its uses as a home computer it was by no means an asset in the classroom. The amount of time spent trying to work out how to operate the new gadget was totally unjustified. In any case, what possible use is one such machine amongst upwards of thirty pupils? We did our best.

Primary One

After teaching at the middle stages for several years I returned to Primary One. How different from my very first class. Although, even at this time, there was no nursery assistance, many of the children were already five years old and most had spent some time in a pre-school nursery or had at least attended a playgroup. The children were phased in gradually over the first week or so, with just a few of them attending at any one time, which meant there was a chance to get to know them as individuals and so build confidence. For the next few weeks, until

October, the children attended only half days. Peripatetic teachers for PE and Music were involved and parents would offer to help at such times as getting ready for PE. The day ended earlier for pupils from P1 to P3.

All things considered the whole situation was much more easily managed than that which I experienced in the inner city school in England.

There were two Primary One classes in this school year to which children had been assigned randomly and not according to age. I worked closely with my colleague in the other class ensuring that the same themes were covered throughout the year. Sharing ideas and supporting one another was refreshing: we were not in competition.

The Japanese Boy

In this class was a Japanese boy. The family had just arrived in Scotland from Japan. The mother was Japanese and the father Scottish, but Japanese was the language spoken in the home.

This was a new challenge for me but I need not have worried. The child was very bright, and in amongst a class of English speaking children he was soon to learn. I gave him no extra tuition but simply monitored his activities at regular intervals ensuring that he had plenty of opportunity to 'play' with just one other child. In a group, he would stand apart, watching and listening. With one individual he would join in: the English speaker would chatter away, quite soon to be rewarded by English responses. It was quite amazing to see the progress. By Christmas, not only was this boy fluent in English, he was in the top reading group. When I spoke to his mother to thank her for her support she said that she had done nothing. Her son still only spoke Japanese at home, adamantly refusing to converse in English. So, everything that the boy had learned was a result of his interaction with the other children in the classroom and the playground.

Primary One / Primary Two

For a short time at the beginning of the following year, before going on secondment, I had a composite Primary 1/2 Class.

Bobbie

One of the P1 boys, Bobbie, had some serious behavioural problems. From reports gained via his Nursery these problems were well documented. His attention span was limited, he was hyperactive and generally quite 'wild' though, I would have to add, he was likeable; there was no malice in him. Though certainly a problem, it was difficult to be cross with him. One day, whilst painting at an easel, he managed to daub himself in black paint. It was everywhere. His clothes were covered, his face and hands were black and his hair was matted. I took him over to the sink and cleaned him up as best as I could, even rinsing his hair. What a mess!

Since I was to be leaving shortly, the teacher who was to take over the class came along to help out and get to know the children. Being a composite class she would take one of the year groups whilst I had the other. This, of course, made the job of teaching so much easier. One day Bobbie came up to me and said, "I think this is a very good idea, we should have two teachers all the time." He was so right.

I was to meet up with Bobbie again when I was teaching Primary Four a few years later.

CHAPTER 14

Secondment (DPSE)
(Diploma in Professional Studies in Education)

In 1988 I applied and was accepted for a one-year secondment to the College of Education to study for a postgraduate diploma. There were eleven other teachers from throughout the region on the course, all very fortunate to have the chance to study without the added responsibility of teaching full time. It was a superb opportunity to review educational practice with the benefit of years of experience, to share ideas with fellow teachers and to be able to observe individual children in our 'placement' schools.

Observing Children in the Nursery

We were all assigned to schools with a pre-school nursery, which we visited throughout the year whilst engaged in a variety of projects. It was a sheer delight to be involved in case studies within the classroom without having to manage the whole class and it proved to be a most interesting exercise in understanding children's behaviour. It is a pity that all teachers cannot engage in a similar experience after a few years class teaching.

Observing how children were able to cope in the nursery environment was a real eye-opener. The skills they could master at the end of the year was quite amazing, but the real lesson for me was the fact that these same children lacked such competence when entering the primary one class just a few weeks later. Taking children out of their 'comfort zone' and setting them in a strange environment appeared to have an adverse affect on their ability. For the first few weeks they did not function at the level they had achieved in the nursery class.

This is, of course, a lesson for us all as it can apply equally to adults entering a new workplace. It also applies to pupils making the transition from primary to secondary school. I have come across secondary school teachers in despair with pupils entering their first year in the secondary school who seem to have learned nothing. It can appear that primary schools are not functioning properly. Not so. It would be a worthwhile exercise for secondary teachers to observe just what these children are capable of at the end of their primary seven year. Naturally they are going to need time to adapt to their new secondary school environment, but given a few weeks they should be back up to standard and ready to move forward.

....

Studying the behaviour of young children can be intriguing. It is often thought, for instance, that they are unable to see things from someone else's perspective, but I noted several examples when this did not appear to be the case.

As I worked with children in the Nursery I became very much aware of their ability, even at this stage, to play together in a collaborative way, to take on the identity of characters in role-play situations and, in a variety of ways, to consider others.

I was most interested to discover the intentions of one boy who appeared, on the surface, to be 'attention seeking' and generally making a nuisance of himself. However, on watching him intently over a thirty-minute period I realised that he was, in fact, making attempts to involve his peers in collaborative play. His attempts were, on this occasion, ultimately successful, and resulted in several children coming together and building a wall. This was followed by an amusing role-play situation with a little assistance from the nursery teacher who simply supplied them with a bundle of newspapers. The whole group became tired workers with their feet up 'at home' (the book corner) reading newspapers and watching television.

Another child, Victoria, frequently behaved in a vary positive way towards her peers offering helpful suggestions, usually in the context of creative 'art' work such as drawing, painting or collage. When I asked Victoria to make a special picture for me she began to draw a house. A few moments later she asked if my house had stairs. I said that it did not but that there were several steps leading up to the front door. A little later she asked what colour my car was. I told her that it was blue, but she wasn't satisfied and wanted to know what sort of blue it was. I took her over to the window from where she could see the car. She was delighted, completed the picture and gave it to me explaining that she had drawn my house with my car in front of it.

Throughout my years in teaching I came across many children who would be regarded as 'bright' but I only ever came across one child who could be considered 'gifted' and it was in this nursery. At four years old this little boy appeared to be able to read anything. His mother insisted that she had never attempted to teach him but that somehow he taught himself. It was truly amazing. One day I took him through to the library and randomly selected a book. Without any problem he was able to read. I asked how he knew what was written. He looked at me completely puzzled and simply spelled out some of the individual words, as if I was the one who needed help. He was, I should add, not sounding out the letters but naming them, so he was obviously not learning to read phonetically. It was fascinating and totally baffling.

One afternoon I had gathered a group of children around me to talk about how they came to school, whether walking or by car. We also talked about some of the things they passed on their way to school. When this very clever little boy returned to nursery the following afternoon he handed me an envelope. Inside was a piece of paper on which he had drawn a map showing the route he had walked to school. He was able to explain in great detail the directions taken from the moment he left his home until he reached the nursery.

It is quite thrilling to come across a child with such ability but it is also quite worrying, for the implications are far reaching. It is so important that children are engaged with their own peer group, a necessary prerequisite for their social and emotional development. But how does a gifted child fit in academically with other children of their own age? Sadly, I did not have the opportunity to follow this child's progress throughout his education.

Apart from the opportunity to study children in the Nursery, some time was also spent in P1 to P3 classes when I opted to focus on number work including an in-depth study: translation from concrete to abstract. It gave an enlightening insight into how children think and learn and was so valuable when returning to a class of my own. In one instance, a Primary Three class had been working on subtraction. One of the girls had completed a problem very quickly so I asked her how she had worked it out. She gave me a lengthy explanation in which she tried to tell me how she thought she should have done it, i.e. the way she had been taught. I knew that she could not have done it that way so I challenged her. Defeated, she finally described the method she had actually used. As on other occasions, when it came to arithmetic the children who struggled, really struggled, but others found their own strategies. It is perhaps a stark reminder to us all that children often have their own ways of working things out. So often in primary school classrooms I have come across children who have been criticized by their teacher as they attempt to devise their own methods: the most typical perhaps, "don't count on your fingers". Well, honestly, what could be more natural!

CHAPTER 15
Back to School

Computers and the New Curriculum

The year's secondment was a refreshing experience and provided a whole new outlook when returning to school. Although an early stages class was not available the focus on young children had important implications for the other stages in the primary school. So, with a Primary Four class I was armed with a plethora of ideas, easily adaptable to this stage.

It was quite surprising to see how things had changed during my one-year absence. A major improvement, we now had the facility to make copies of teaching materials, thus easing the burden of having to produce our own work cards. But, not all things were simpler.

Computer technology had moved on, although primary schools were and continued for many years to be the 'poor relations' as regards access to new machines. We had to make do with computers passed on from local secondary schools or donations from industry as they purchased newer ones. Technology was moving at an incredible rate and it seemed that we were continually left behind. The newer machines were certainly an improvement on the Sinclair model but by no means ideal. Further, we only had rare access to technicians and then only by request. It really was hopeless.

How did anyone expect a whole generation of teachers brought up on slate boards and pen and ink to cope unaided with all this new technology?

The Computer Training Farce

Finally some computer training was offered: I was the one member of staff from our school sent on a one day training course to the college in the city, some thirteen miles away. It was an incredible palaver because, at that time, computers were still relatively new to education. Each person attending this course had to take their own class computer to the college. In my case the janitor was summoned to dismantle the machine and carry it from my first floor classroom, down the stairs, along a corridor, across the playground to the car park where it was deposited into the boot of my car. On arrival at the college another janitor had to be sought and the machine manoeuvred out of the boot, around the outside of a building, up a flight of stairs and into the room where the in-service training was to take place. A technician was then called to connect up all of the machines: a much more complex process than would be required with our more modern computers.

Once each computer was set up and tested the training could begin. A young woman, a supposed computer 'whizz-kid' with just two years experience in teaching, was the designated tutor. We were to learn how to use a particular computer program to set out the front page of a journal. The whole morning was spent conjuring up suitable headlines and articles. This became almost a competition as to who could dream up the most original stories for their page. This was definitely not the purpose of the day. Finally, in the afternoon, we were guided as to how to arrange our headlines and articles on the said page.

I was appalled: The purpose of the day was to promote our skills in the use of the computer, not to spend half this precious time showing off our creative writing skills. Articles etc. should have been made available at the start of the morning so that we could immediately begin to learn how best to organise the content.

At the end of the day the whole fiasco of transporting the computers back to our respective schools was undertaken in reverse.

As a follow up to this training course we were then to adopt an approach known as 'snowballing' in order to pass on our newly acquired skills to the rest of the teaching staff (in my case about ten). Part of an in-service training day was set aside for this purpose.

Occasionally a member of staff was sent to another school for a few hours to gain some knowledge of a specific program from colleagues who had found something useful, but this was rare.

As may be deduced from above, the whole process of introducing computers into the primary school was totally unsatisfactory.

Primary One
Computers and Primary One

Computers, as stated, were becoming ever more significant, yet teachers still had little or no training and most did not have a computer at home. We really were muddling our way through. Not so, our youngest pupils. Faced once again with a new intake, it was intriguing to see how children of the 'up and coming' generation were already familiar and comfortable with our fast developing technology. Most were from homes where the computer was already a familiar feature or where they had been introduced to technology in the form of games accessed by devices connected to a television. It was quite amusing to witness the reaction of these youngsters to the computer in the classroom:

They were totally un-phased by it. Without any reservations they would hop up on the stool in front of the machine and could already master some keyboard skills.

Having the time to observe them I soon discovered that it was a good way for them to learn the relationship between lowercase and uppercase letters. They would very quickly realise that the uppercase letters on the keyboard came up on the screen as lowercase and that they must press the shift key to produce the initial letter of their name. At a later date special keyboards were produced for primary school pupils showing just lower case letters. Having observed these Primary One pupils, as described, I regarded this as a lost opportunity.

Philip

In this Primary One class I faced a very difficult challenge in the form of a boy called Philip. At barely five years old he was much bigger and very much tougher than any of the other children in the class. Disastrously, he had a temper to match. From the point of view of some of the very much smaller girls in the class he must have been a 'thug'. He would frequently 'lash out' at them, totally unprovoked. On one occasion he brought his hand down with a thud onto the back of the hand of a girl who was sitting at a table drawing. The situation came to a head with one particularly nasty occurrence. On his way back to class from a visit to the toilet he took it upon himself to go into the other Primary One classroom. He approached a girl who was painting at an easel and swiped her hard across the face. A few minutes later the other Primary One teacher came to my room with the victim of this abuse, the vivid red marks of Philip's fingers showing clearly on her cheek.

Soon after this incident, with an ever-lengthening list of cruel attacks to his name, I felt that I could no longer cope with his abusive behaviour. In desperation I committed my fears to paper, concluding that Philip's actions were such that they represented a serious danger to the other children, and for this reason I was no longer prepared to accept responsibility for him in my class. On receipt of this written statement the Headteacher took immediate action: Philip was removed from the school straight away and a place found for him in a special unit that same day. It was only after this episode that I discovered Philip had been excluded from three Nurseries before starting school. His mother, a teacher herself, came to see me and to say 'thank-you'. Both parents had been desperate for help for their son, being especially concerned for the safety of his younger sister. I'm not sure how long Philip attended the special unit but he did eventually return to school: I taught him again in Primary Five.

....

It was during this school year in Scotland that the 5-14 Guidelines were about to descend with a vengeance, accompanied by National Testing and Targets. Teachers were required to spend 50 hours a year on Personal Professional Development as part of their contract. Some of this time was taken up with Planned Activity Time (PAT), usually an hour each week at the end of a school day. In connection with the developments, as indicated below, my time with this Primary One class was curtailed.

CHAPTER 16

Curriculum Development Officer

It was 1990. I was again offered a secondment, this time working for the Region as a Curriculum Development Officer. This was essentially an advisory role, supporting primary school teachers in the implementation of the 5-14 Programme (the new curriculum guidelines in Scotland). I had responsibility for English Language.

On my first day in the job I had to report to Education Offices some 60 miles away where a real farce was about to unfold. A Regional Advisor, another secondee and myself met to discuss the implementation of the new guidelines. Together we were to run a teachers' in-service day later that same week based on the new English Language document. Problem. We didn't have a copy of the final document, just a draft. We managed to 'cobble' something together, but for me it was a real eye-opener: life on the other side of the fence. Just a few days earlier I had been in the classroom, now I was expected to deliberate to other teachers how to implement guidelines that were not yet available.

On the day of the in-service the documents finally arrived, sufficient copies for each of the teachers present and for the three of us. Surprisingly, the day went well but it was a nerve-racking experience. Things did improve. We became familiar with the documentation and subsequently visited many schools throughout the Region as well as leading several in-service days.

The majority of schools visited were small two teacher schools in rural areas. It was in these that the Headteachers appreciated the kind of help and support we were able to give. Implementing the new guidelines was an onerous task and having to run a school and teach several stages was no mean feat. I saw my role as practical. Going into a school to observe and comment was, to my mind, not an option.

A Small (Two-Teacher) Rural School

The Headteacher of this school was very innovative and eager not to be out-phased by the new documents. In her teaching she was well organised but was struggling to keep her small office in order. There were so many magazines and booklets but she never had the time to get them sorted. I had a plan. Together with her small group of Primary Seven pupils I discussed how we could rearrange things. With a little input, the children themselves devised a system, and over three or four sessions sorted everything in alphabetical order. They were delighted to work in their Headteacher's office and motivated to be involved in a task where their efforts were acknowledged and praised as practical and worthwhile. In discussion with the Headteacher we identified how many aspects of the curriculum had been covered in carrying out this useful work. It was surprising as well as satisfying.

Another 'mini-project' in this school was the creation of a small garden: the planning process for this venture involved much thought and negotiation. A fund raising event was organised, an expert called upon, plants purchased, and once completed, an 'open' event was arranged to which parents were invited and the children talked about their part in the venture. As well as 'Environmental Studies' this exercise once again took account of much of the English Language Curriculum.

Tackled in this way the new curriculum became much less daunting.

A School of Seven Classes in a Housing Estate

The Headteacher in this school was due to retire at the end of the term. An elderly, spinster lady who had taught 'forever', she loved her job and the children. She also had a 'thing' about frogs. Her room was filled with ornaments of frogs of all sizes. The teachers on the whole were unimpressed by her eccentric ways but the children loved her. They were in awe of her bizarre collection and over the years made many contributions.

Towards Christmas the children were involved in the preparation of a special concert for the pending retirement, to be held in a nearby church hall. The teachers, however, were worried about the pressure they were under to cover the work in the English Language curriculum: how would they manage to 'tick the boxes'? Christmas was an unwelcome interruption.

When we are totally immersed in the classroom it can be difficult to see exactly what is going on. Faced with a mountain of documents and associated paperwork the whole situation can become too much. Being on the 'outside,' having time to read and understand the guidelines, meant it was possible to make sense of the documentation in terms of classroom practice. In an advisory capacity I was thus in a position to step back from the responsibility of being in charge of a class and was able to assess the situation from a different perspective. With time to reflect it was amazing just how much of the curriculum was being covered incidentally in the midst of all the activity. Many boxes were ticked.

Comment:

In large schools teachers can discuss and share ideas with

each other. In the smaller schools the support I was able to give in this 'advisory' role was genuinely appreciated.

Sadly this secondment, originally planned for two years, was cut short after just one year through lack of funding. I was privileged to have had the experience and it proved a real advantage when returning to the classroom myself.

CHAPTER 17

Back to School Again
Acting Depute Head

On returning to school I was asked to take on the role of Acting Depute[4] Head. With a composite Primary 3 / 4 class and the help of a supply teacher one day a week in order that I might undertake duties demanded by this position, it was one of the most satisfying years of my career. The children were amazing and the knowledge I had gained during the previous year gave me much confidence. I was given the responsibility for the in-service training of the staff with whom I had an excellent working relationship. This involved the planning and preparation of in-service days as well as the weekly Planned Activity Time.

Bobbie

The one difficult child in this class was Bobbie, the same boy I had already taught at the beginning of his first year. His attention span had not improved over the years, and although he had been identified by each of his teachers as presenting a problem, he had not yet been assessed.

Bobbie frequently arrived at school with far more junk food for break time than was acceptable. I spoke to his mum who instructed me to confiscate any such items: she would provide him with some fruit. However, he still managed to sneak packets of crisps into school, which were duly extricated and placed in a cardboard box on a high shelf in the cupboard, to be returned to his mum at a later date. The whole thing became somewhat of a

---

[4] In England this would be 'Deputy'.

game to him, for he made no attempt to hide them from me once in the classroom and would often come and hand me the offending items without being asked: I strongly suspect that he was trying to see how many packets of crisps would end up in the box.

Eventually, an assessment by an educational psychologist was arranged and a visit pending. I was informed that the psychologist would attend for a whole morning to observe Bobbie's behaviour in the classroom. On the appointed day the lady arrived in my room just as the children were settling down. After approximately five minutes, without a word to me, she disappeared and reported to the Headteacher. Shortly afterwards the Headteacher appeared in my room to say that the psychologist had concluded that Bobbie was fine: the teacher was the problem! In utter disgust he had seen her off the premises. A week or so later, when the dust had settled, she reappeared to assess Bobbie on a one-to-one basis. The child was subsequently recognised as requiring help and a place in a special unit was found to accommodate him. Oddly, in this case, I was rather sorry to see him go.

The Seaside Trip that Nearly Wasn't

Things are seldom predictable when working with children, but sometimes working with adults can be equally unpredictable. One day a coach load of us set off to the seaside, or at least that was the intention. As we turned out of the school gates I thought it strange, for the driver was taking us in the opposite direction from the way I would have thought the most direct. However, I assumed he must know what he was doing. Once out of the village I began to feel a little uneasy. Several miles along country roads and I was convinced that something was very wrong: we were definitely heading inland. Eventually I approached the driver and whispered, "You do know we are going to the beach?"

"No," he replied, "I thought this was a mystery trip".

Another Bus Fiasco

One afternoon, just as the Headteacher had left the building leaving me in charge of the school, as well as my class, the secretary rushed into my room in a panic. She had received a telephone call from the Education Office. They had decided, in their wisdom, that the bus company that transported the 'country' pupils to and from school should lose their contract, taking immediate effect. This decision, coming as it did in the middle of a school day, resulted in absolute chaos; a situation, which must have been replicated throughout the Region. We were left to get in touch with a parent or contact person for each of these children to let them know that there would be no transport for their children that afternoon and to try to make alternative arrangements. Had those sitting behind their desks in the education office any idea of the impact of their rash decision?

Towards the end of the year one of the girls in the class approached me and commented, "Do you know, Miss, you're always smiling." It reminded me of a piece of advice given when on my initial teacher-training course: "However you are feeling always welcome the children with a smile." I hope I managed to convey this message to the students I encountered during the next two years of my career as a lecturer at the college, training prospective teachers and running in-service courses for teachers.

CHAPTER 18
New Innovations

By this stage in my career many things had changed in education and further changes were taking place. We had already been bombarded with new technology in the form of the computer. Paperwork had increased at a phenomenal rate and several forests must have been demolished to produce the mass of documentation with which we were confronted. But preceding all of this, other innovations had already been encountered along the way.

The Initial Teaching Alphabet

The Initial Teaching Alphabet (ITA), introduced in the early 1960s, was a system designed by Sir James Pitman (grandson of the man who devised Pitman's shorthand), in order to help children to read more quickly. A further 14 letters were added to the original 26 letters of the Roman alphabet to represent sounds such as 'oo' and 'th'. Only the lower case letters were used.

This was a logical idea in theory bearing in mind that 13% of English words are not spelt the way they sound. It all made some sense; it provided a spelling system where all words were made up of speech sounds; it was phonetic.

However, apart from the fact that a whole range of special reading materials had to be produced, serious snags arose as pupils switched to the standard alphabet and spelling at the age of seven. Although some children managed, others encountered real problems and struggled thereafter with the English spelling conventions.

The school in which I spent the first $6^{1}/_{2}$ years of my career was considered for this scheme and I have to comment that I, along with my colleagues, were relieved when this proposal was dropped. Instead we were confronted with 'Breakthrough to Literacy', a scheme with its own problems as indicated earlier.

a	ɑ	æ	au	b	c	ch	d
apple	arm	angel	author	bed	cat	chair	doll
ee	e	f	g	h	ie	i	j
eel	egg	finger	girl	hat	tie	ink	jam
k	l	m	n	ŋ	œ	o	ω
kitten	lion	man	nest	king	toe	on	book
ω	ou	oi	p	r	ɼ	s	ʃh
food	out	oil	pig	red	bird	soap	ship
ʒ	t	th	ŧh	ue	u	v	w
treasure	tree	three	mother	due	up	van	window
wh	y	z	ʒ				
wheel	yellow	zoo	is				

The Initial Teaching Alphabet (ITA)

Open Plan Schools

In the 1960s and 1970s the concept of the 'Open Plan' school came into vogue. I first came across one such school in the course of my initial teacher training. The establishment in question was a school in a mixed social area with quite a high immigrant population. The purpose in this instance was to organise the teaching such that three teachers shared the workload of three classes, a whole year group, with one teacher taking responsibility for English, another for Mathematics and a third for others areas of the curriculum. The staff appeared enthusiastic to be a party to this new innovation, but I found it difficult to see any real advantages: it seemed all too open and noisy with more distractions than existed in a conventional classroom.

However, somehow the idea seemed to 'catch on' as, subsequently, many new schools were purpose built in an open plan style. Throughout my career as a classroom teacher I succeeded in escaping this arrangement. In one school where I was employed for two years the main school was built in this fashion but I occupied a classroom in one of the 'huts' in the playground. The school itself was totally open, often described by colleagues as a big barn, with no divisions except those created by a few low bookshelves at the edge of a class area. Teachers needed to co-ordinate their teaching so that the use of shared resources and a 'quiet room' could be utilised effectively.

I would have to comment that I have never been convinced of the supposed value of the open plan classroom. It seemed to me that it was a money saving exercise. There are plenty of distractions for young children in a normal classroom without sharing an area with several other classes. Some schools did have part-dividing walls, which made them just about acceptable, but others were so cramped that the classes spilled over into each other. In some the classes were even in 'walk-ways', constantly disturbed by children, teachers and visitors passing through, circumventing the desks and the chairs on their way. In one instance, when I was a tutor visiting a student, the only available place for me to sit in order to observe the lesson was a children's table in the next class. I can't think how any such scenario can possibly enhance the education of our children. Maybe someone can enlighten me?

The Integrated Day

Another innovation was 'The Integrated Day'. This approach took on different forms and undoubtedly meant different things in different schools, although similar in that it veered from the traditional approach being less formal and allowing pupils a certain ownership of the curriculum.

In some situations the focus was on the integration of the different subject areas by utilising a particular project or theme: a topic based approach covering all areas of the curriculum. In other situations the focus was on an alternative organisation of the school day, where the individual subject areas remained clearly identifiable. Perhaps, more usually, it was a mixture of both.

The teacher would set up a series of workstations each focusing on a different aspect of the curriculum. The pupils would then choose which 'stations' to visit. Although allowing certain freedom of choice a monitoring system would be in place such that each child covered all areas of the curriculum over a specified period of time, perhaps a week.

I did witness one example where an integrated day, for a time, proved successful:

A former colleague for whom I had a great deal of respect was appointed Headteacher of a small country school where I had, for one term, spent some time as a supply teacher. It was a two-teacher school with two classrooms. On the appointment of the new head the wall between these two rooms was demolished to make one very large room. Workstations were established to cater for the needs of all children from Primary One through to Primary Seven and the two teachers worked across the whole area. With low pupil numbers (less in the whole school than would be found in one average sized class) the system was working extraordinarily well. I was most impressed with the smooth running of the school, the enthusiasm of the staff and the response of the pupils.

About a year later I met with my friend and asked how things were going. I was rather surprised to learn that she had had to abandon this method and return to a more formal approach. "Why?" I asked. Well, the school had become so popular that families, who had previously opted to send their children to the larger primary school in the nearest small town, now favoured this small country school. The number of pupils therefore increased to the extent that the integrated system became unmanageable. I was disappointed that this way of working ultimately proved too much of a challenge for someone as talented and dedicated as this Headteacher. A serious message for us all: this progressive idea maybe all right in theory but with normal class sizes it is simply not practicable.

Phonics

This was not a new innovation, but judging by the amount of publicity expended in the tabloid press during the 1990s one may have been forgiven for thinking that our politicians had just invented it. There was a constant barrage of criticism of primary school practice and an urge to promote phonics as the answer to all the problems of teaching reading. From the moment I set foot in a classroom I had always acknowledged the value of teaching phonics but never to the exclusion of other methods employed in the teaching of reading. This old 'gem' by an unknown author highlights the reasons why:

```
I take it you already know
of tough and bough and cough and dough?
Others may stumble, but not you
on hiccough, thorough, slough and through.
Well done! And now you wish, perhaps,
To learn of less familiar traps?

Beware of heard, a dreadful word
That looks like beard and sounds like bird.
And dead; it's said like bed, not bead.
For goodness sake, don't call it deed!
Watch out for meat and great and threat,
(They rhyme with suite and straight and debt)

A moth is not a moth in mother,
Nor both in bother, broth in brother.
And here is not a match for there,
Nor dear and fear for bear and pear,
And then there's dose and rose and lose
```

--
Just look them up -- and goose and choose,

And cork and work and card and ward
And font and front and word and sword.
And do and go and thwart and cart --
Come, come, I've hardly made a start.
A dreadful language? Man alive,
I mastered it when I was five.

CHAPTER 19

Lecturer In Primary Development

For a third time I was offered a secondment and for the next two years I was employed as a lecturer in a college of further education (now a faculty of the university) where students attended a four-year course leading to the Degree of Bachelor of Education. A further remit was to support teachers throughout the Region who were involved in post-graduate studies. The post also entailed producing documentation and leading in-service training in order to support teachers in the implementation of the vast array of materials that constituted the 5-14 Guidelines. It was an interesting and enlightening experience affording contact with a whole range of primary schools, a 'bird's-eye view' of what was happening in schools throughout an entire region. These included traditional and open-plan, inner city, urban and rural, large and small, independent and state, all used as venues for student placements. One school had a high proportion of disabled children, several of whom were confined to wheelchairs. It was an enriching time for me as well as for the students.

Another part of the remit as a college lecturer was 'Personal Professional Development' for which a proportion of time was allocated. In a higher education establishment the concept of the learning process as one that continues throughout life is an important feature. In this respect I decided, and was encouraged, to study for the Degree of Master of Education, ultimately involving some research necessitating contact with local education offices and more schools: an exercise in diplomacy as much as anything considering the already overstretched responsibility of headteachers. Participating in a survey is often the last thing that busy individuals are prepared to make time for.

Without the pressures of a class commitment it was a delight to observe and reflect on the changing face of education. It is also, however, easy to get carried away and have raised expectations of what is feasible for the individual classroom teacher to achieve. In producing the Guidelines in Scotland and The National Curriculum in the rest of the UK one has to wonder just how much classroom experience the initiators of these documents had: how far removed from reality they were. Common sense certainly did not prevail.

Take, for example, the Religious Studies Document. Primary School teachers were somehow expected to equip pupils with knowledge of five major religions: Christianity, Judaism, Islam, Buddhism and Sikhism. By the 1990s most teachers barely had a grounding in Christianity: attendance at Sunday school, once the norm for most children, had long since disappeared from the agenda as part of family life.

Environmental Studies was unmanageable by any stretch of the imagination. Several attempts at the production of this document reverted back to 'the drawing board'. Quite how many forests were swallowed up in this process beggars belief. And the proposal mapped out in the final document was still unachievable.

Admittedly, guidelines for primary teachers were required in order to bring about some standardisation throughout the country, but the documentation produced went way beyond what was necessary. The burden of so much paperwork was overwhelming, so that rather than providing genuine support it left many teachers feeling inadequate. Promoting children's education, giving them the best deal is what matters, rifling through a mountain of directives and ticking an unprecedented number of boxes is surely counterproductive.

Undergraduates, on the other hand, had not known anything different: they were coming into teaching from a different perspective. The Guidelines were their starting point, offering them a structure, a framework upon which to base their practical experience. Neither were they completely ignorant in the field of computer technology, so they were much more prepared for the progress with which they would be faced at the beginning of their careers during the 1990s.

Of course these students were still confronted with the many challenges of teacher training. There are one or two highlights that come to mind:

One mature student was assigned a middle stages primary class for a teaching practice and had chosen to read to the children a popular Roald Dahl story, 'Danny, the Champion of the World'. Danny and his father, who repairs cars, live in a gypsy caravan and as a hobby poach pheasants. In connection with this the student had invited into school the local gamekeeper. (A sensible choice to put the idea of poaching into perspective as perhaps not such a good idea in reality.) However, at the last moment the gamekeeper was unable to attend so, without consulting either the school or the college, the student brought in a poacher! The Headteacher was subsequently faced with a barrage of angry parents and the college duly informed. The whole incident caused quite a stir.

Another student was unable to face the fact that the work she produced, although usually very good, did not, in the eyes of her tutors, always match her own expectations as exclusively grade 'A'. Nothing less was ever going to suffice. When, on one occasion, she was awarded a 'B' for an assignment she was furious and complained bitterly. The said assignment, apart from being assessed by myself, had also been assessed and confirmed as a 'B' by another tutor. There was nothing she could do. Towards the end of the course students were given forms on which to make comments about the tutors. These were meant to be anonymous but this student wrote very distinctively using green ink and was positively rude about any tutor who had dared to challenge her work as less than perfection.

Mostly, the experience in the college was very positive. The students were enthusiastic, they had embarked on training for the teaching profession by choice and were receptive and respectful. Lecturing to a whole year group was somewhat daunting but the rest of the experience I found refreshing and rewarding.

PART 4

A NEW CHALLENGE

CHAPTER 20

The Private Sector

Shortly after completing the two-year secondment at the college I was appointed Head of the Lower School (i.e. Primary and Nursery) at an all girls independent school. This was a completely new experience for me in the course of my career, although there were many similarities with the grammar school I had attended as a child. Here was a totally different regime, an ethos where learning really mattered to the pupils, encouraged by parents who invested much in the way of effort as well as finance in the future of their daughters. The Lower School was part of a whole school catering for pupils from Pre-school Nursery through to the Sixth Form. The Nursery included boys as well as girls but from Primary One upwards it was girls only. The pupils in the Pre-school Nursery and Lower School together often outnumbered those in the Upper School with up to ten classes in the Lower School alone.

All prospective pupils and their parents were warmly welcomed and given a tour of the school. The children of those expressing an interest in a place were assessed for entry. The main intake was the start of the school year in August, but by nature of the location there was a constant stream of new entrants joining throughout the year, as families were re-located from around the world. Within the Primary School the assessment of prospective pupils was the responsibility of myself with the support of the Marketing Manager (herself a former primary teacher and also a former pupil of the school). We worked closely together in the welcoming and introduction process.

The catchment area for the school, unlike a state school, was not limited to the immediate surroundings. Originally the school had accommodated boarders but by the time I joined the staff it was a day school only. Consequently, many pupils travelled from distances of up to 40 miles each day, including children in the primary department - a long day for a young child. The majority of families were relatively well off although an increasing number, being disillusioned by state education, were making huge sacrifices in order to give priority to their children's education.

For a school covering the entire age range it was relatively small, lending itself to the family atmosphere, which was always promoted as a positive feature of the school. Assemblies were a regular occurrence bringing pupils together. At least once a week children from Lower Three upwards joined the Upper School for this purpose, adding to the 'family' effect.

Classes were small and manageable, and I would have to acknowledge that the absence of boys was an asset to the education of the girls.

Although not class committed I did take classes on a regular basis. Free from the distractions so often encountered in state schools, and with children who were so eager to learn, the whole experience was a real joy.

Despite this somewhat rosy picture the private sector did not come without its challenges:

The parents, having invested so much in the education of their offspring, were extremely demanding. Liaising with specialists from the Upper School, all of whom were keen to promote their own subject throughout the school, could be time consuming. Peripatetic music teachers, who taught a number of instruments, required to take pupils out of class lessons for tuition: this would often prove frustrating for teaching staff.

On one occasion a parent telephoned the school early in the morning, before the start of the school day at 9 a.m., claiming to be in the company of a number of other parents and a newspaper reporter. She accused the school of neglecting pupils by not providing supervision for those who arrived at school before the start of the school day. I explained that we did provide supervision for children who required such provision from 8 a.m. onwards - at a cost. This did not suffice. She wanted to know what happened to pupils arriving in the playground early - why were we not supervising them - why could they not come into school and go directly to their classrooms? I had to emphasise that legally the teaching staff could not be held responsible for pupils until the start of the school day, that up until that point children were the responsibility of their parents or guardians.

Another parent, who maintained that her child was being bullied, demanded to observe the children in the playground. After much deliberation this was granted but only discreetly and under strict supervision.

Although not living in poverty the children, as everywhere, had their own specific problems. Parents making demands on the school were also making demands on their children. Expectations were high: for some too high. In learning to read, for example, parents would too readily compare their child's progress with that of others in the class forgetting perhaps that the age range within a class amounts to a whole year, aside from the fact that children learn at different rates. I came across one family in which the parents wanted their daughters to be way ahead in their computer knowledge and skills. These girls were staying up at night through to the small hours to play computer chess with 'friends' in America.

Many children had an incredibly demanding timetable out of school hours leaving little freedom for independent pursuits and play.

The Former Pupils' Association made an award each year for the pupil in her final year in the Upper School with the best all round achievement, including extra-curricular activities. The list of achievements was invariably so exhaustive that I wondered that any one thing could have been done to an acceptable standard.

Double Tragedy

Towards the end of the term before I took up my appointment in the school two sisters, one in Primary Five and the other in the Nursery, had lost their mum to cancer: obviously a very sad situation. A short time later the father of another girl in the Nursery was killed in a tragic accident in Russia. Both of the Nursery girls continued on to Primary One and 'found each other'. On several occasions when prospective pupils and their parents, or other visitors were brought to the Primary One class, these two girls would rush to the door announcing, "My mummy's dead", "My daddy's dead": an embarrassing situation which just had to take its course - so very sad.

Cutting the Tie

One day, towards the end of the afternoon, two girls, who were in trouble, were sent to me by their class teacher: the ultimate punishment. One of the girls had dared the other to cut her school tie. So the child did just that. I reprimanded both girls equally. They went away very shame-faced. At the end of the school day the mother of the child whose tie had been cut came to me in a rage. Why had I reprimanded her daughter when it was the other girl who had cut the tie? I would have thought the answer to that was obvious! Had the girl's tie been cut in an act of callousness or bullying, then of course, but when she had deliberately invited the misdemeanor I concluded that they were both equally to blame. What probably made the situation worse was the fact that the child who had done the cutting was the daughter of one of the teaching staff. (Nothing is ever simple). Some time later the initially angry parent approached me to apologise, saying I had been quite right in my response to the incident.

The Glass Eye

A girl in a Primary Seven class had, very sadly, lost an eye and was therefore provided with a glass eye, which from time to time came out: Quite a trauma for the girl in question, if not just a little disconcerting for her classmates. This girl had a sister in the Primary Four class. One day the Primary Four teacher had asked her class to tidy up. She told them to pick everything up that was lying on the floor. Two of the girls were scrambling about under a table when one remarked to the other that it reminded her about looking for a glass eye. The other child happened to be the younger sister of the girl in P7 with the glass eye and the teacher, just catching a part of the comment, immediately jumped to the conclusion that she was referring to this girl's sister: she was angry and brought the child to me. The child in question seemed genuinely unaware of any wrongdoing. She explained to me that she had been referring to a book that she had been reading about someone who had a glass eye, describing the story in some detail. The girl was only eight years old and I doubted that she had made up this story. I explained the problem to her but she was obviously very upset to be reprimanded for something that she clearly did not understand.

A Thief in our Midst

Loose change, items of food etc. began to disappear from coat pockets and bags in the cloakroom. I spoke to the girls in the class that appeared to be at the centre of the problem but failed to identify the perpetrator. Then one morning a parent came to me to reveal her concern. She lived quite close to the school and a friend of her daughter's was coming to her house each morning so that the two of them could walk round to the school together. The parent had observed that things had started to disappear from a table in her hallway. Since she had not actually caught the child in the act she did not want to make any false accusations, but she was sure that it was her daughter's friend. Hearing the rumours about other items missing from school she had decided to make her concerns known to me. On questioning the girl the whole truth came out. I spoke to the child's mother, who was in fact a member of the administrative staff in the school, and the matter was dealt with sensitively, without a great deal of fuss. It seemed that the problem was a cry for help. The girl had a younger sister whom she saw as getting an unfair share of attention. This sibling was away on holiday abroad with her grandparents and the older child was feeling left out. The parents were thus alerted to a problem to which they seemed totally oblivious.

Emily

Emily joined the Lower School in Primary Seven. She suffered a form of growth deficiency, a condition which had also resulted in severe curvature of the spine. In consequence she could not participate in all of the physical activities nor was she able to carry her schoolbag. The normal classroom chairs also presented a problem for her as, thus seated, she was unable to reach the desk in order to read or write comfortably. However, these problems were not insurmountable. She could easily hop up onto a high stool and the girls in her class were more than willing to carry her school bag and any other belongings. Emily was one of the most delightful girls I have ever had the pleasure to meet. Apart from being bright, of above average intelligence, she was always cheerful and positive. She continued through to the Upper School and on to university. I met up with her several years later when she was employed in a department store between leaving school and going to university.

Paula

Paula presented a very sad case. She also joined the school in Primary Seven. Suffering some brain damage, possibly as the result of a tumour, she would sometimes collapse or have a fit and have to be admitted immediately to hospital. In her previous school she had been the object of much bullying. I was reluctant as to how she would manage, and it was indeed some time before she settled. Often she would remain in the playground after the bell following playtime or the lunch break. However, the other girls cared for her and eventually won her confidence. Sadly, as a result of her medical condition, Paula did not survive to adulthood.

Nadine

Nadine joined the school in Primary Six. Her mother alone was raising her: they had recently moved to the area from

Glasgow. It was obvious that the mother wanted the best for her daughter and was working very hard to achieve this goal. However, it was clear from the start that Nadine just did not 'fit in'. Regarding her behaviour, she lacked the discipline that was so inbred in the majority of the girls: her background was completely at odds with her peers. Her mother worked in an office almost a mile away from the school and she expected her daughter to meet her there after school. This should not have been a problem for an eleven year old as the route was fairly busy with pedestrians. However, Nadine had other ideas. Stubbornly she took to simply staying at the school, refusing to move. She could have attended our 'After School Club' but it was obvious that the mother was not prepared to incur this added expense when her daughter was quite capable of walking to her mother's office. The problem was, she just wanted to be like the other girls, the majority of whom were deposited and collected from school by their parents. It was a constant battle, sometimes alleviated when other parents would offer her a lift, but which was only finally resolved when she reached the Upper School and many other girls were then expected to walk to and from school themselves.

So, as can been seen, not all was plain sailing. Independent schools are often much more concerned about retaining their place at the top of the league tables than in accepting individual pupils who may not quite fit the bill. But the challenge presented by the pupils as mentioned above offered the girls an invaluable lesson in the real world. A challenge to which they rose with patience and kindness providing lessons in life, which cannot be taught within the normal curriculum.

Assessment for Entry

Although prospective pupils were assessed for entry to the school it was only rarely that a pupil was turned away. Many of the girls in the school were of above average ability but there was always a significant minority who were average or slightly below. These were children with whom we could cope and they were more than welcome. It was a joy to see how they progressed and eventually went on to be accepted for higher education: these were the children for whom we really made a difference.

We did, however, have to acknowledge in the assessment process that from time to time a child just did not meet the criteria. The reason for this: although we had a learning support teacher in the school we did not have access to special units that were, at that time, a facility provided by the Region. In the case of children with specific needs, state schools were able to refer them to such units, sometimes long term or sometimes just for part of the week, as deemed necessary. Since we were not in this position there were children who would be better catered for within the state system.

Privileged

In general terms the girls in this school, despite any individual problems, would be considered privileged. One of my first duties, having taken up the position as Headteacher, was attending a small gathering of the Lower One and Two classes for their first assembly of the new school term following the Christmas break. I was quite astonished to learn how far afield some of them had travelled to celebrate the festive season. Later I learned that it was quite normal for parents to go over to New

York for a couple of days to do their Christmas shopping.

Visits and excursions out of school were a regular feature, but in the Upper School these tended to be far more adventurous than I had come across in the state system. For instance, each year a group of skiing enthusiasts would head off to the continent or even the USA led by a number of keen teaching staff. About 18 months prior to taking up my appointment a group of secondary school pupils had gone to Australia on a school trip! This whole experience was far removed from the experience of my first teaching post in which pupils had no knowledge of a world beyond their own concrete jungle: clearly I had landed on a different planet!

The Lower School, though rather less adventurous, were often involved in short visits linked to an aspect of the curriculum. In addition, towards the end of the school year the Primary Seven pupils had a few days away on an 'Activities Week'. On two occasions I accompanied them. The first time was memorable and ultimately rather amusing. We were to stay at a Christian Adventure Centre by the side of Loch Tay. Since our total complement of Primary Seven girls was insufficient to fill the available places we were to be joined by pupils from a school in another city. It was not until we arrived that we became aware that these children were from a mixed school in a deprived area. They could not have been further removed socially from our privileged group of girls. I have to say that I was somewhat alarmed at the prospect of a week with such a diverse combination. However, for the most part, the groups were segregated and led by different qualified staff from the Centre in the various activities on offer. When the groups did come together in the evenings we were amused to see the interaction between our relatively 'mature' Primary Seven girls (at 12 years of age some were already physically well-developed) and the rather juvenile and 'rougher' boys from the other school. It seemed that our girls 'fell in love' with them, much to the annoyance of the girls from the other school who displayed not a little jealousy at the attention given to 'their' boys. Despite this potentially volatile situation the week passed without major incident, a good time being had by all. Before leaving, some of our girls exchanged addresses and invited the boys to come to visit them. In fact, I doubt that anything transpired: there were certainly no repercussions. I need not have worried.

Behind the Scenes

Being involved in school management can be a real eye-opener: some of the things going on behind the scenes, yet vital to the smooth running of the whole establishment, really were unbelievable.

Missing Mail

A young girl was appointed to assist the school secretary, taking on board some of the routine duties involved in the day to day running of the school. Following her appointment a problem arose in respect of outgoing mail. Parents of prospective pupils would get in touch to question why written confirmation of an offer of a place had not been received. In each case the offer had, to our knowledge, been forwarded. Both the Marketing Manager and I raised this issue independently but nothing was done. When this situation continued and it became apparent that other items of mail were not reaching their destination we were suspicious that outgoing mail was not being posted. We expressed our concerns but were both told not to be so ridiculous. There was no way that the mail was not being posted. The assistant secretary was taking it out of school at the end of each afternoon so, 'what else could she possibly do with it?' The answer came a few days later when a resident in the neighbourhood close to the school found bundles of mail dumped in his garden shed, accessed from the back lane nearby. The young culprit was dismissed on the spot.

Unfit for Purpose

The facilities in the Pre-School Nursery were in a poor state, the kitchen, for example, being unfit for purpose to the point that it was a health hazard. I expressed my concerns to the school governors who investigated with a view to rectifying the problem. An architect, a friend of one of the governors, was consulted and asked to provide an estimate for the installation of a new kitchen. A cost of over £6000 was quoted to carry out the necessary work. The governors decided that this was far too much so declined to meet the cost. I'm sad to say that the Nursery was not a priority.

About a year later the government proclaimed that nursery education should be made available for all children in Scotland in their pre-school year. Since the local authorities did not have sufficient places within the state schools they looked to the private sector to accommodate the shortfall. It was decided that, with government funding available, we would accept some of these children. However, this meant that our facilities had to be of an acceptable standard as identified by regional guidelines. It was the very last week of the summer term before we were furnished with these guidelines and, unsurprisingly, the facilities in our Nursery did not match the criteria. The work necessary to bring the Nursery up to speed had to be completed before the start of the new school term and it was too late to consult the governors. The plans for the kitchen drawn up the previous year were resurrected, the janitor was informed and this wonderful man together with his assistant, a retired joiner, were sent out, with the approval of the bursar, to purchase the necessary components from the local B & Q store. Before the end of the holidays a new kitchen had been installed at a cost of a little over £600. I will refrain from stating the obvious!

To Return to the Curriculum

Although subject to inspection by HMI, the same as any state school, the private sector had always retained its own agenda and high standards. When aspects of the curriculum such as rote learning, including the chanting of the multiplication tables, became unfashionable in the state system, private schools ignored the trend. When local authorities reclaimed school playing fields, mostly to be sold on as building land, the private schools held on to theirs. Exercise, including competitive sports, was never compromised. In the school where I spent these latter years of my career, music and art also played a significant role, and although drama was not on the main curriculum, dramatic performances were a feature, with staff dedicating their time during lunch breaks and after the end of the school day.

My appointment as Head of the Lower School was very much as a result of the experience and expertise I had gained in my involvement with the implementation of the 5-14 Guidelines during the Regional Secondment and the two years I had spent in the College. Whereas staff in the state sector had devoted many hours of Planned Activity Time (PAT) and In-service to these documents, including discussion and workshops, teachers in this school had been left to their own devices and were feeling somewhat left out. If they ever wanted to advance their careers this would leave them at a disadvantage. When I arrived at the school, curricular policy documents were in need of a serious revamp to bring them up to date. This was something I was able to do, as was supporting the staff in the practical application of these guidelines.

Generally, Language and Mathematics were manageable. Expressive Arts, covering PE, Art and Music was supported by specialist teachers in the Upper School who were largely responsible for these areas of the curriculum within the Lower School. Regarding Religious and Moral Education, in discussion with the staff, it was decided that in addition to Christianity we would tackle just one of the other major religions. Since Islam was to be a main focus in the Upper School we decided to focus on Hinduism. In addition I agreed to undertake a series of lessons on Judaism with the Lower Six and Seven classes. To expect primary school teachers to tackle five major religions was really not feasible. Environmental Studies was generally tackled through project work although, to fulfill all the expectations as set out in the document, was just not possible. Information and Communications Technology (ICT) now played a much more significant role in the primary school curriculum. There were computers in every classroom and access to a computer room where whole classes could be involved in mastering particular skills. The Lower School was in a fortunate position in this respect, being able to access expertise available in the Upper School.

Another directive from the government was the proposal

that headteachers should observe and assess their teaching staff. This was something of which I really did not approve. Teachers are professionals, they have already been through this process in the course of their training and to scrutinise their professionalism in this way is simply not acceptable. Besides, to spend precious time sitting at the back of a classroom is surely counterproductive. Why not go in to a class to participate, to be of some practical assistance? This will have exactly the same results in ascertaining a teacher's strengths and weaknesses and provide a much more positive starting point for discussion should any serious problems emerge.

In many ways the private sector offered a completely different perspective within the education system although, as in the state sector, there are undoubtedly vast differences from one school to another. In my experience a significant advantage was the value placed on education by all parents, not just some or even the majority. Investing in their child's future was important to them and in many cases this meant making choices both financial and in terms of time. In turn, this was reflected in the pupils' attitude towards learning: it mattered to them.

Private schools have never strayed from acknowledging the importance of the expressive arts, physical exercise and sports. Because the Lower School at which I was Headteacher came under the canopy of the whole school we had the advantage of expertise in these areas from the staff in the Upper School whose remit and skills extended to the younger classes.

Extra-curricular activities also remained an important aspect in the private sector contributing to the all-round development of the child. Even activities undertaken totally outwith the remit of the school were recognised and encouraged.

Traditions such as frequent assemblies and the Closing Ceremony at the end of the school year have remained valuable components, which, however archaic they may seem, serve as a bond giving pupils a sense of belonging.

SUMMARY

During the 1950s and 1960s and even into the early 1970s at the start of my own teaching career, the emphasis in primary schools was on the 3 R's: 'Reading, Writing and Arithmetic'. Religious Education was and still is compulsory. P.E. lessons played a part in the curriculum but children had plenty more exercise walking to and from school and going out to play. Nutrition was, 'eat it or go hungry' although in general children enjoyed a well-balanced diet free from the mountains of junk foods and sweets 'inflicted' on future generations.

Through play children socialised with their peers free from interruption by adults. They learned to interact with each other, to invent, to become independent in their thinking. Children respected their parents and their teachers. The classroom was a place to settle down to work, there was a no-nonsense atmosphere where general chatter was not tolerated. Resources were limited to the reading scheme books, which were often old, tattered and in limited supply. Primary school teachers produced their own work cards for the pupils and also made much use of the blackboard from which children would copy out their work. Curricular issues were rarely discussed amongst staff although there were certain expectations as pupils progressed through the school.

During the 1970s changes began to take place. As the years of the post war era slipped by, class sizes decreased, facilities improved and materials became more abundant. Workbooks for Maths and Language began to appear on the market to support the work of teachers in infant and junior departments. The Degree of Bachelor of Education gradually became the more popular option for teacher training until, by the early 1980s, it was requirement for new teachers in the whole of the United Kingdom, replacing the old Certificate in Education (Cert Ed). This undoubtedly raised the profile of primary education. In order to provide further support for practicing primary school teachers the Open University introduced courses to enhance understanding in areas such as reading and language development. Primary and eventually Nursery Education began to enjoy an improved status within the education system.

During the 1980s commercially produced materials continued to increase. New and more attractive reading schemes were introduced along with associated support materials. Photocopiers became available in primary schools so that teachers were able to select and reproduce photocopiable materials that now flooded the market.

The introduction of the computer into the primary school made a massive impact but for the first few years at least, with no support for staff, this was more of an intrusion than an asset.

It was the 1980s into the 1990s that the biggest changes took place in primary schools with the introduction of the National Curriculum in England, Wales and Northern Ireland and the 5-14 Guidelines in Scotland. Although the latter was supposedly less prescriptive, the introduction of testing in English and Mathematics at different stages together with set targets seemed to suggest otherwise.

Being bombarded with so many initiatives caused much frustration within the teaching profession. Certainly, some things did need to change, but to be inundated with such an abundance of material was overwhelming. Attempting to fulfill all of the requirements of the 5-14 documents and the assessment and reporting that went along with them placed an unrealistic burden on teaching staff. Indeed the associated bureaucracy created a 'paper mountain': absolutely everything had to be recorded.

Attaining targets and performing well in league tables was not too much of a problem in the private sector, but having results reported in the national press and naming and shaming schools where pupils presented much more of a challenge seemed cruel and demoralising. The children in the school, which was my first teaching post, could never have matched the attainment of the girls in the private school where I spent the latter years of my career, yet my colleagues in that state school worked tirelessly to ensure that those pupils who did have the potential were given the best opportunity.

Over the decades there were other initiatives that, I am sure, emerged from purely economic considerations, for example, open plan schools.

Studies by educational psychologists instigated new ideas in methodology: group teaching, individual programmes of learning, the integrated day etc. Research has concluded that children's learning can improve given these ideals but ideals they are. Applied to individual pupils they may work very well but given the whole class situation it is a totally different matter.

In the past, although opportunities for physical education within the school day may have been limited, children at least enjoyed the freedom to go out to play. In addition, it was not uncommon for local authority schools to have playing fields but, over the years, many have been lost, sold off for housing developments.

Over the past 35 years more than 10,000 school playing fields across Britain have been turned over to development: the legacy of which is a generation of

children prone to obesity and diabetes.
The Telegraph 12th September 2014

As if the potential medical outcomes of this shocking policy to rid our children of vital opportunities to exercise were not bad enough, the educational implications are far reaching.

Throughout this period the way in which children were being brought up was changing. The increase in traffic meant 'going out to play' was much less a feature of everyday life, as was walking to and from school unaccompanied by adults. Televisions, electronic games and computers were replacing traditional games and interaction with peers. For many children school had become the one place where they had the opportunity to socialise, to establish friendships. The classroom too had changed, pupils being expected to talk and listen as well as read and write. Practical work and problem solving played a more significant role and children were encouraged to make choices. The computer had become an important tool in the learning process.

However, as a result of all the changes, it would appear that children tend to be under much more pressure than in the post war era. Modern living has, to a large extent, denied them their own time and space.

By the time I reached the end of my teaching career in 2001 computers were a familiar feature in all primary classrooms and some schools were running pilot programmes issuing pupils with their own laptop computers. Pupils with special educational needs were already being furnished with their own laptops in order to provide support for their specific difficulties.

Since leaving the teaching profession technology has continued to move on at an incredible pace with many children fixated on 'tablets' almost before they have learned to walk. The computer, no longer a simple resource within the classroom, is now a link to the outside world providing pupils access to the internet with its wealth of information spanning the globe. However, it is also a breeding ground of misinformation, presenting untold dangers to the vulnerable at the press of a key.

Comment:
Despite all the challenges, I consider myself very fortunate to have had the opportunity to teach and especially to have had such a varied career within the teaching profession. Though not without their problems, the children were a delight, no matter their background, whether rich or poor, deprived or privileged, from inner city or remote countryside: to encounter such a cross section was truly amazing. It provided a wealth of experience as well as a collection of wonderful memories. I was also privileged to spend time on secondment, both in an advisory capacity and as a lecturer in a College of Education, to be able to study and to learn as my career progressed.

Those entering the teaching profession in the 21st century are already immersed in the technological era, thereby equipped to tackle what was for my generation a serious burden. Teaching is a vocation; it requires dedication as well as skills and expertise, but most of all a genuine desire to care for, to understand and to educate our young people.

About the Publisher

'For The Right Reasons' is a charity in Inverness set up to help people who want to conquer their drug or alcohol dependency. It aims to give them unconditional, un-judgemental support and friendship throughout the whole process, from the time they make the personal commitment to get clean or dry, to the day they can re-integrate with society.

In order to help achieve their goal the charity provides purposeful employment in running a charity shop, a gardening scheme and a publishing and printing enterprise.

Rev. Richard Burkitt, founder member and director of the charity, which started in 2007, continues to work relentlessly to support those in need.